本丛书系教育部中外语言交流合作中心 2021 年度国别中文教育调研项目:"一带一路"背景下与牙买加共建中文国际学校的可行性研究(项目编号:21YHGB2008)、牙买加中文教育的历史与现状研究(项目编号:21YHGB1036)、"一带一路"背景下面向牙买加的国际中文在线教学资源建设研究(项目编号:21YHGB2007)的相关成果。

"百人百译" 丛书编委会

总 顾 问：张晓阳

总 主 编：冯 雷 张金萍

本 册 主 编：马建军 叶如钢

本册副主编：杨秀波 王成杰 王 毅

编　　　委（按姓氏拼音首字母排列）：

蔡铁勇 曹小菁 丁后银 丁如伟

董庆瑗 董秀静 何 艳 乐国斌

李开林 李 治 马建军 任诚刚

王成杰 王 婷 王 毅 吴春晓

伍敏毓 杨秀波 杨中仁 叶如钢（美）

袁浩龙 张俊锋 Reana Davis（牙）

Grace Liu（加）

国粹经典『百人百译』丛书

总主编 冯 雷 张金萍

名言警句英译

主编 马建军 叶如钢

暨南大学出版社
JINAN UNIVERSITY PRESS

中国·广州

图书在版编目（CIP）数据

名言警句英译/马建军，叶如钢主编. —广州：暨南大学出版社，
2023. 10

（国粹经典"百人百译"丛书／冯雷，张金萍总主编）

ISBN 978 - 7 - 5668 - 3779 - 0

Ⅰ. ①名… Ⅱ. ①马…②叶… Ⅲ. ①汉语—格言—英语—翻译
Ⅳ. ①H136. 33②H315. 9

中国国家版本馆 CIP 数据核字（2023）第 178247 号

名言警句英译
MINGYAN JINGJU YINGYI
主　编：马建军　叶如钢
....

出　版　人：张晋升
策划编辑：杜小陆
责任编辑：康　蕊
责任校对：黄　颖　王燕丽　黄亦秋
责任印制：周一丹　郑玉婷

出版发行：暨南大学出版社（511443）
电　　话：总编室（8620）37332601
　　　　　营销部（8620）37332680　37332681　37332682　37332683
传　　真：（8620）37332660（办公室）　37332684（营销部）
网　　址：http：//www. jnupress. com
排　　版：广州良弓广告有限公司
印　　刷：广州市金骏彩色印务有限公司
开　　本：787mm×1092mm　1/16
印　　张：22. 25
字　　数：290 千
版　　次：2023 年 10 月第 1 版
印　　次：2023 年 10 月第 1 次
定　　价：95. 00 元

（暨大版图书如有印装质量问题，请与出版社总编室联系调换）

总　序
Preface

　　隽语，短而智、简而美，启发心智、陶冶情操、耐人寻味，是民族品格、思想、智慧和审美的集中体现。中国是文明古国，更是文化大国。她的名言警句、谚语俗语和经典诗词，是文化箴言，是中华民族的群体记忆和文化标识。英译、分享这些箴言，是中国文化走出去的重要途径，对中西方之间加深了解、理解，避免误解、误判，意义重大。

　　隽语负载文化特色，是民族思想和思维模式的反映，同时也是文化交流障碍和翻译难点。中国文化名言浩如烟海，大量值得译播。我们精选内容积极向上、语义独立完整、表达优美、传播广泛的短句作为翻译题目，进行"一题多人多译"。因"译无定法"，不同译者即使对同一译题解读相似，译文也常有各自的特点。

　　本系列丛书是"百人百译"中国文化名言项目的主要成果。本项目通过译者团队、中方评判团队和外籍评判团队实施。译者团队包括国内高校英语教师、各行业精通英语的人士、定居欧美的高学历华人华侨等。中方评判团队以国内高校英语教师为主。外籍评判团队包括在国内高校工作的外籍英语教师、留学生和海外人士。译者中英双语俱佳，背景各异。译文丰富多彩、各具特色。隐去译者姓名后，译文提交给两个评判团队征集反馈。获一名中方成员认可的译文标注一个"●"，外籍成员认可的译文标注"★"，接受度一目了然。在三个团队的共同努力下，截至2022年底，我们完成了五百多条名言警句、六百多条谚语俗语和150多首诗词或诗词片段的英译及评判反馈工作，积累了数百万字的原创语料。

评判团队成员也是译文的首批读者，他们的反馈告诉我们：第一，产生共情是获得读者认可的深层因素。如果原文含义与译文读者有共情，译文越贴近原文，接受度越高；无共情，则结果相反。第二，读者背景影响译文的接受度，并呈现多维化。对同一译文，读者的生活经历、知识结构、艺术感悟不同，则判断不同。以语言文化背景为例，部分外籍团队成员不懂原文含义，多以表达的清晰度和流畅度为判断标准，即便译文偏离原文，也无从知晓。中方读者理解原文，对译文的判断往往是"字面上的忠实度"。第三，译者在翻译过程中会出现"盲区"，因两种语言和文化互相干扰而影响对译文的判断，正所谓"身在此山中，不识真面目"。从这个角度看，"双语双文化"本是优势，有时反成劣势。第四，译者的翻译标准与读者的评价标准有摇摆性。埃兹拉·庞德（Ezra Pound）于 1915 年出版他所译的十二首李白诗，选用了自由体。后来他不断学习汉语，几十年后翻译《诗经》时却采用了韵体。同样，对中诗英译，不通中文的读者，常只以内容和诗意衡量译文优劣。通过学习，有了基本的中国诗词格律知识后，他们的评判标准会有所改变。中英双语读者对译诗的判断，则取决于自身的中英诗歌知识和修养。

我们精选"百人百译"成果的部分内容以飨读者。在此特别感谢暨南大学出版社的支持。原创译文和对"一题多译"的反馈是"国粹经典'百人百译'"丛书的两大特色。入选译文均得到了中外评判团队的认可。很难讲有完美的翻译，但出现不少有如神来之笔的"佳译"和"妙译"。丛书完整呈现了对译文反馈的原始记录，这对翻译学习者、实践者和研究者均有重要价值。

特此鸣谢上海大学赵彦春教授在项目实施之初的大力支持。马建军、吴春晓、叶如钢、曹小菁、任诚刚对本文写作和修改提出了建议；王成杰、杨秀波、丁如伟、董秀静等协助润色了文字。

冯　雷　张金萍

2023 年 5 月

名言警句英译

前　言

Introduction

　　名言警句，是指一些名人的著名言论，以及富有内涵的警示话语。这些言论形式简练而含义深刻，蕴含着丰富的人生哲理，是对生活、对世界的提炼和总结，例如"谦受益，满招损""学而不思则罔，思而不学则殆""老吾老以及人之老，幼吾幼以及人之幼"等。许多名言警句流传千古，乃金玉良言，掷地有声；像智慧火种给人启迪，像灯塔指引方向，像启明星在暗夜里闪亮。可以说，名言警句是中华传统思想文化的精湛表述，也是中华民族的智慧结晶。因此，名言警句英译是一项非常有意义、有价值的工作，能助力传播中华优秀传统文化，向世界展示中国文化之精妙。

　　本书为国粹经典"百人百译"丛书第一册，从"百人百译"国际翻译平台精选 230 条名言警句的多版优秀译文，以飨读者。与其他名言警句英译词典相比，本书具有以下特点：

　　一是考量名言警句的经典与流行。230 条名言警句由"百人百译"团队 15 名译者从"百人百译"国际翻译平台 502 条精心选择的名言警句中投票选出，内容上力求广泛，贯通古今，上至先秦时期，下至近现代时期；既涵盖经典文化，如诸子百家、史书典籍、唐诗宋词，又包括通俗流行文化，如小说、戏剧、散文、小品文、对联、家训等。

　　二是考量译文的多样性，即一题多译。名言警句虽然有迹可寻，却独立成句。在理解和使用时，既要考虑其出处，充分理解其原始含义，也要考虑随着名言警句的频繁使用，时代所赋予的新的含义。

因此，本书每一条名言警句列有若干优秀译文，几条到十几条不等，而不是仅仅提供一条译文。这些不同的译文呈现出不同的表达风格和个性，提供对原文的多角度诠释，为有不同应用目的的读者提供多种选择。

三是考量译文的读者接受度。入选优秀译文经外方评委和中方评委投票选出，充分体现翻译研究中对读者接受度的考虑。读者接受度是指翻译文本符合译入语的构词造句方式和表达习惯，为译入语读者所理解和接受的程度。随着翻译研究的重点从文本导向转向了读者导向，读者接受度也成为衡量译文质量的主要标准之一。本书入选译文获得中外评委不同程度的青睐，从而为译文质量提供了强有力的保障。同时，每条译题后均附有投票评委人数，保留入选译文投票信息，从而提供直观的读者接受度。译文按照得票多少排序，一颗星表示外方评委一票，一个点表示中方评委一票。票数相同情况下，有星有点的译文在先，主要是考虑这样的译文既有信度又有流畅度；其次是只有星的译文，最后是只有点的译文，因为名言警句英译的主要目的是对外传播，外方读者是译文的主要受众。

四是考量翻译策略的多样性。本书所选名言警句一般短小精悍，承载丰富的中国特色文化。在精选译文时，既考虑异化策略，通过直译法保留原文中传统中国的经典意象；又考虑归化策略，通过意译法直接陈述名言警句所蕴含的哲理；还考虑通过转译法，选择使用目标文化中的经典意象来取代原文的中国意象；也考虑直译和意译结合的方法，在保留中国意象的同时，还阐释其哲理。这些体现不同翻译策略的不同译文，结合其读者接受度，既可以为读者展示不同译文之精妙，也可以成为读者研究翻译策略的极佳语料。

本书名言警句按年代划分，共五篇。第一篇为先秦时期，精选诸子百家和四书五经中的经典名句，体现孔孟老庄等先贤思想。第二篇为秦汉魏晋南北朝时期，名言警句多出自史书典籍，如《礼记》《史记》《战国策》《后汉书》等。第三篇为唐宋时期，名言警句多出自唐诗宋词以及唐宋八大家的散文，如李白、杜甫、白居易、苏轼、陆游、韩愈等名家作品。第四篇为元明清时期，名言警句多出自小说戏剧，如《红楼梦》等四大名著、《醒世恒言》《初刻拍案惊奇》《张孔目智勘魔合罗》等，以及《增广贤文》《菜根谭》《小窗幽记》《格言联璧》等小品文集。第五篇为近现代时期，精选蔡元培、鲁迅、胡适、华罗庚等近现代名人的经典名言。本书最后还提供了作者/著作索引和句子索引，方便读者查阅。

本书由马建军和叶如钢担任主编，负责整体设计和样章编写；冯雷和张晓阳负责方案和样章的审核。编撰工作具体分工如下：叶如钢负责第一篇的编辑工作，杨秀波负责第二篇的编辑工作，王成杰负责第三篇的编辑工作，王毅负责第四篇的编辑工作，马建军负责第五篇的编辑工作。此外，伍敏毓和曹小菁参与编辑第一篇，马建军参与编辑第二篇和第三篇，刘群参与编辑第三篇，袁浩龙参与编辑第一篇和第三篇，李开林和李治参与编辑第四篇，李开林和袁浩龙参与名言警句作者和出处的审校工作，董秀静、伍敏毓、袁浩龙、丁后银和杨中仁参与其他校对工作。借此书稿付梓出版之际，谨向各位编者表示由衷的谢意。

尽管本书编写力求精确、完备和实用，但是受编者水平所限，难免挂一漏万；书中翻译不足之处也在所难免，敬请同行专家和广大读者不吝批评赐教。

以翻译讲好中国故事，以翻译促进中华文化对外传播，这项任务艰巨、充满挑战，我们将继续踏实前行。

马建军　叶如钢

2023 年 5 月 18 日于大连、圣巴巴拉

名言警句英译

目录

名言警句英译

Contents

第一篇
先秦时期

Chapter I
Pre-Qin Period

【1】 德不配位，必有灾殃。——《周易·系辞下》

投票：外方评委7人投票★，中方评委5人投票●

1. Power, if not guided by virtues, is bound to incur disasters.

（石永浩 译1） ★★★★★★●●●●

2. A person occupying an important position but with no integrity will have to face his own doom.

（李开林 译） ★★★★●●

3. Calamities befall those who hold power but do not deserve it.

（石爱伟 译） ★●●●

4. An immoral power is doomed for calamity.

（樊功生 译） ★★★

5. Lacking morality and ability for his position, he shall sooner or later suffer big misfortune.

（董庆瑗 译） ●●●

6. If one's moral character doesn't correspond to the position he holds, both he and his job will be harmed.

（冯雷 译1） ★●

7. Powerful but not virtuous, one is doomed to fall.

（石永浩 译2） ●●

8. Those whose virtues do not match their positions are doomed to bring about catastrophes.

（倪庆行 译） ●●

9. A dishonest ascent leads to a destructive end.

（冯雷 译2） ●●

10. One will suffer for sure if his status doesn't match his moral character.

（张晓阳 译） ★

名言警句英译

【2】 安而不忘危, 存而不忘亡, 治而不忘乱。

——《周易·系辞下》

投票：外方评委5人投票★，中方评委9人投票●

1. In times of peace, prosperity and order, be alert to signs of danger, downfall and disorder.

（王如利 译）★●●●●●●●●

2. Beware of danger in security, of fall in power and of turmoil in order.

（艾朝阳 译）●●●●●●

3. Danger may come when you feel safe; death may come when you are alive; turmoil may come when everything is in order. So always prepare for threats and challenges.

（冯雷 译1）★●●

4. A country should always be alert to perils, destruction and turbulence even in times of peace, well-being and stability.

（许霖越 译）★●●

5. In peace be aware of perils; in existence be aware of extinction; in governance be aware of chaos.

（王绍昌 译）★●

6. Forget not perils while things are peaceful, forget not extinction while things are in sound existence, forget not turmoils while things are in great order.

（叶如钢 译）★★

7. In safety we should not forget danger, in existence not forget destruction.

（任诚刚 译）●●

第一篇　先秦时期

8. Be alert to peril in peace, death in survival, chaos when stable.

（张琼 译）●●

9. Rulers should bear in mind that perils are hidden in security, downfall in survival and chaos in peace.

（赖祎华 译）●●

10. Even if a state survives, is controlled and safe, the ruler should be fully aware of the possible danger, turmoil and fall that bring calamity to its people.

（冯雷 译2）★

11. While enjoying peace, do not forget possible perils; while celebrating survival, do not forget danger might be at your heels; even when the country is well governed, stay vigilant about latent turmoils.

（王昌玲 译）★

12. Keep danger, downfall and disturbance in mind in time of safety, survival and stability.

（华卫 译）★

【3】天作孽，犹可违；自作孽，不可活。

——《尚书·商书·太甲》

投票：外方评委10人投票★，中方评委7人投票●

1. Man can survive natural disasters but can't get away from his blunders.

（魏红霞 译）★★★★★★★★●●●●

2. What one may survive is a natural disaster, but what one can't is his blunder.

（杨中仁 译）★★●●

3. A natural disaster is irresistible, but a man-made one is unforgivable.

（艾朝阳 译）★●●●

4. One may escape from a natural disaster, but he has to reap what he has sown.

（石爱伟 译）●●●●

5. Natural calamity may miss you, but you reap what you sow.

（王昌玲 译）●●●●

6. Man can prevent from thunder, but can't forgive self-made blunder.

（郁序新 译1）●●●●

7. We may escape disasters the nature has brought, but man-made calamities we will survive not.

（冯雷 译）★★★

8. Don't do evil, or you'll deserve it.

（彭智鹏 译）★●

9. A man-made disaster is more horrifying than a natural one.

（樊功生 译）★★

10. Humans can dodge natural disasters but not human-inflicted tragedies.

（王绍昌 译）●●

11. A person may avert an unexpected disaster, but he will invite death by his own wrong-doing.

（杨秀波 译）●●

12. Man can flee from natural calamity, but cannot be rid of a self-caused mishap.

（郁序新 译2）★

13. You can survive natural disasters, but not self-inflicted ones.

（张顺生 译）★

【4】满招损，谦受益。——《尚书·大禹谟》

投票：外方评委6人投票★，中方评委8人投票●

1. Modesty makes you gain, while conceit brings you pain.

（铁冰 译）★●●●●●●

2. A modest man gains and a self-conceited man loses.

（石爱伟 译）★★★★●●

3. Humility brings benefits, conceit invites harms.

（刘群 译）★★★●●

4. Being modest, you go ahead; being complacent, you fall behind.

（曹小菁 译）●●●●

5. From humility, we will benefit; as a result of complacency, we will incur a deficiency.

（段冰知 译）★★●

6. Modesty brings gains, complacency incurs losses.

（冯雷 译）●●●

7. Modesty rewards, while conceit does the opposite.

（石永浩 译）★●

8. Humble, you gain; conceited, you lose.

（樊功生 译）●●

9. Humility helps; arrogance hurts.

（王绍昌 译）●●

名言警句英译

【5】行出于己，名生于人。——《逸周书·谥法解》

投票：外方评委 10 人投票★，中方评委 5 人投票●

1. Virtue originates from within, but fame from others.

（杨秀波 译）★★★★★★★●

2. Good conduct brings good name.

（王成杰 译）★★★★

3. Fame is given but actions are self-driven.

（王梅兰 译）●●●●

4. What one has done decides what fame he will have among others.

（张晔 译）★●●

5. Your deeds are what you're done; your fame is who others think you are.

（铁冰 译）★●●

6. You decide what to do; others decide who you are.

（王毅 译）★●

7. Do good not to seek fame, but to give meaning to your life.

（刘向军 译）★★

8. Take good care of your obligation, and others will take care of your reputation.

（石永浩 译）★●

9. Humans, do thine and shine!

（王绍昌 译）★

10. Do the best you can and leave it to others to honour you with a title you deserve.

（叶步青 译）★

11. Whether you behave nobly depends on you. Whether you achieve a reputation depends on others.

（张小琴 译）★

【6】投我以木桃，报之以琼瑶。——《诗经·卫风·木瓜》

投票：外方评委8人投票★，中方评委6人投票●

1. A favour owed is to be returned.

（石爱伟 译）★★★★★★★

2. My love shares with me a peach so delicious; I present her with a gemstone so precious.

（石永浩 译）★★●●●

3. On accepting your juicy peach when extremely thirsty, I give you my jade as a token of everlasting friendliness.

（杨秀波 译）●●●

4. A sweet peach for me, a pure jade for thee, only thy love heart I always see.

（郁序新 译）●●●

5. When I got anything, in need, I would return plenty indeed.

（王绍昌 译）●●●

6. In return for the papaya you bestowed, I'll repay you with a precious jade.

（倪庆行 译）●●

7. Your peaches are so sweet and dear to me, and I have to give you a precious jade to show how much you mean to me.

（叶如钢 译）●●

8. A peach you gave me sweetens my lonely heart, and the jade I return you emblems your pure mind.

（杨中仁 译）●●

9. Precious for precious, heart for heart.

（李开林 译）★

名言警句英译

【7】 道阻且长，行则将至。

——语本《诗经·国风·蒹葭》《荀子·修身》

投票：外方评委9人投票★，中方评委6人投票●

1. No road is long and rough for a man strong and tough.

（王成杰 译）★●●

2. Our life is a long journey full of challenges. We must keep going to a-chieve our goal.

（冯雷 译）★●●

3. The road ahead is long and hard；embark on it and the destination will be reached.

（何艳 译）★★★

4. Though the road is long and obstructed，keep going and you'll arrive at the destination.

（叶如钢 译）★●

5. The way to success is long and full of frustration，but so long as we keep moving on，we'll finally reach the destination.

（董秀静 译）★●

6. The path may be long and arduous，but if you persist in traveling it，you will reach the end.

（杨胜悦 译）★★

7. Though the road ahead is hard and long，we'll reach the destination as long as we keep marching on.

（张晓阳 译）★

8. Patience and perseverance inspire us to go forward in the arduous path to success.

（郁序新 译）★

9. Every start brings an arrival even though the road ahead is arduous and long.

（马建军 译）★

10. The journey is long and full of hurdles. Continue moving forward and you'll get to where you want to be.

（王梅兰 译）★

11. The road is long, but not too long.

（李开林 译）★

【8】所谓伊人，在水一方。——《诗经·国风·蒹葭》

投票：外方评委 4 人投票★，中方评委 3 人投票●

1. The one I love is beyond my reach.

（王梅兰 译）★★

2. The girl I admire is there beyond the river.

（杨秀波 译）★★

3. My fair lady's across the river beach; alas, she's so close but beyond reach.

（刘雪芹 译）●●

4. Oh my bonnie lass, she's on the other side of the river.

（曹小菁 译）●●

5. The bonnie lass that I much adore is right on the other side of the shore.

（王毅 译）●●

6. That maid of whom I admire, is standing in a water side.

（张立国 译）★

7. The one that I miss is just on the opposite shore.

（杨胜悦 译）★

8. Oh, my lover, you're in the water side. I'm seeking on the river up and down, to endeavor to be at your side.

（任诚刚 译）●

9. My love is right across the river, but I can't reach her though love-sick.

（石爱伟 译）●

10. Oh, the person after my own heart is over there ashore far apart.

（王昌玲 译）●

11. The girl is my dear, on the other side of the river.

（马建军 译）●

12. On the bank of yonder stream, stands the lady of my dream.

（张建惠 译）●

13. On the other side of the river lives my beloved fair lady.

（何冰 译）●

【9】仓廪实则知礼节，衣食足则知荣辱。——《管子·牧民》

投票：外方评委11人投票★，中方评委11人投票●

1. Well fed, people begin to know rites and etiquette; well provided, people begin to know honor and disgrace.

（乐国斌 译）★★★●●●●●●●●●●

2. Only when the granaries are full do people respect rites and etiquette. Only when people are decently fed and dressed can they take honor and disgrace into account.

（倪庆行 译）★★●●●●●●●

3. Full granaries go before the attention to rites and etiquette; sufficient food and clothes come before the sense of honor and shame.

(张俊锋 译) ●●●●●●

4. Well fed, well behaved; well disciplined, well respected.

(王昌玲 译) ★★●●●●

5. Abundance in food brings civilization; affluence in life boots moralization.

(铁冰 译) ●●●●●

6. Well-behaved rests with well-possessed; well-disciplined rests with well-lived.

(赖祎华 译) ●●●

7. Their granaries full, people have manners. Their food and clothes ample, people heed honor and shame.

(叶如钢 译) ★●

8. No food, no manners; no clothes, no honor.

(周鹏 译) ★●

9. Empty stomachs, ragged clothes, how can people talk about etiquette, honor and disgrace?

(任诚刚 译) ★

10. A satiated dog looks gentle, and a clothed dog looks decent.

(艾朝阳 译) ★

【10】圣人择可言而后言，择可行而后行。

——《管子·形势解》

投票：外方评委6人投票★，中方评委2人投票●

1. Wise people choose words before speaking and consider results before acting.

（王慧玉 译）★★★★★●

2. It is after careful consideration that a sage speaks or behaves.

（延芳 译）★★★●

3. A sage always thinks carefully before he speaks and acts.

（马建军 译）★★●●

4. Wise men wait for a proper time to speak and act.

（樊功生 译）★★★

5. A sage thinks twice about what to say and what to do.

（何艳 译）★●

6. The wise always think before they say or do what's right.

（王梅兰 译）★★

7. The wise exercise prudence in words and deeds.

（石永浩 译）★★

8. Saints and sages take stock of the situation before they speak or act.

（吴春晓 译）★

【11】政之所兴在顺民心，政之所废在逆民心。

——《管子·牧民解》

投票：外方评委7人投票★，中方评委3人投票●

1. The success of governance hinges on whether it follows the needs and aspirations of the people.

（叶如钢 译1）★★★★★●●

2. A state thrives when its people's interests are heeded and declines inevitably if their interests are neglected.

（石爱伟 译）★★★★●

3. A regime thrives when in accordance with people's aspirations and collapses otherwise.

（王毅 译）★★★●

4. Governance succeeds when following the will of people, and fails when going against it.

（叶如钢 译2）★★●

5. Governance advances when carrying out the will of the people, but it fails when going against people's will.

（马建军 译）★★●

6. Success or failure of an administration depends on its popularity among the people.

（刘德江 译）★★

7. The success or failure of the governance lies in whether it's oriented by the public interest or not.

（张晓阳 译）★

8. Whether political power flourishes or not hinges upon whether it is in compliance with people's will or not.

（倪庆行 译）●

9. A policy succeeds when it goes with the will of people, but fails when a-gainst it.

(吴春晓 译) ●

10. If for the people, an administration will bring boom; if not, it will meet its doom.

(石永浩 译) ●

11. Good rule lies in its following people's will, bad rule in against it.

(杨秀波 译) ●

【12】知人者智，自知者明。胜人者有力，自胜者强。
——《道德经·第三十三章》

投票：外方评委 2 人投票★，中方评委 5 人投票●

1. An intelligent person knows others, a wise person knows himself; a strong person can defeat his opponent, a powerful person can discipline himself.

(冯雷 译) ★★●

2. He who knows others is wise, and knows himself is wiser. He who wins against others is strong, and wins against himself is stronger.

(任诚刚 译) ●●●

3. The wiser is he who knows himself more than others, and the stronger is he who can overcome himself rather than win against others.

(艾朝阳 译 1) ●●●

4. It's wiser to know oneself than others; it's stronger to surpass oneself than others.

(曹小菁 译) ●●●

5. A wise man knows others, but a bright man knows himself. A forceful man defeats others, but a powerful winner defeats himself.

（艾朝阳 译2）●●

6. He who knows others is witty. He who knows himself is wise. He who defeats others is powerful. He who defeats himself is strong.

（倪庆行 译）★

7. He's wise to know others but bright to know himself. He's powerful to defeat others but strong to defeat himself.

（陶国霞 译）●

8. Those knowing others are smart, while those knowing themselves are wise. Those surpassing others are strong, while those surpassing themselves are powerful.

（铁冰 译）●

9. A clever man can only know others while a sage can know himself as well; a formidable person can only vanquish others while an invincible person can vanquish himself as well.

（张俊锋 译）●

10. He who knows others is wise, who knows oneself is intelligent. He who defeats others is powerful, who defeats oneself is strong.

（赖祎华 译）●

【13】 道可道，非常道。——《道德经·第一章》

投票：外方评委4人投票★，中方评委6人投票●

1. Dao(The law of nature and justice) can only be partially interpreted. Its essence is totally beyond verbal explanations.

（冯雷 译）★★★●●●

2. Tao is beyond what words can tell.

（李开林 译）★ ★ ★ ● ● ●

3. The ultimate Way cannot be told.

（倪庆行 译）★ ● ● ●

4. The Tao that could be explained clearly is not the ultimate truth.

（杨秀波 译）★ ★ ●

5. The principle that can be articulated is not the Ultimate Principle that governs all.

（王昌玲 译）★ ★ ●

6. Truth can be known, but it may not be the truth well-known.

（任诚刚 译）● ● ●

7. The Dao told or explained is not the eternal unchanging Dao, the Way of the World.

（王绍昌 译1）● ● ●

8. The speakable Tao is not the Tao interpretable.

（艾朝阳 译1）★ ★

9. The told Tao(Truth) is not the Eternal Tao(Truth).

（艾朝阳 译2）● ●

10. The eternal way of universe can only be revered, not interpreted.

（樊功生 译）● ●

11. Any truth that is describable is not the eternal truth.

（铁冰 译）● ●

12. The eternal truth, the Dao, cannot be interpreted nor narrated.

（王绍昌 译2）★

13. The eternal truth possesses inexhaustible possibilities of interpretation.

（石永浩 译）★

14. Tao, the kind of supreme law that you can follow but cannot borrow.

（郁序新 译）★

【14】天之道，利而不害；人之道，为而弗争。

——《道德经·第八十一章》

投票：外方评委 7 人投票★，中方评委 6 人投票●

1. The natural way of Heaven is not to harm, but to help; the best policy for man is not to contend, but to cope.

（冯雷 译1）★ ● ● ● ● ●

2. Heaven's principle is to benefit man without harming, and man's principle is to act without vying.

（王昌玲 译）● ● ● ● ●

3. Heaven helps, not harms; man acts, not fights.

（冯雷 译2）● ● ● ● ●

4. Heaven helps everybody while a sage struggles with nobody.

（魏红霞 译）★ ★ ★ ★

5. Heavenly Way benefits all, without injury; Sages' Way strives, without rivalry.

（王绍昌 译）★ ● ●

6. Heaven is benevolent and does no harm; good men endeavor and are not belligerent.

（叶如钢 译）★ ★

7. The heaven does good but harms none; the sage tries hard but usurps nothing.

（石永浩 译）● ●

8. Divine law favors all without harm; a great man labors for good without hostility.

（郁序新 译）● ●

9. God's way is meant for mankind's welfare rather than its suffering, while man's way is to strive without antagonizing.

（樊功生 译）★

【15】慎终如始，则无败事。——《道德经·第六十四章》

投票：外方评委6人投票★，中方评委8人投票●

1. Prudence at every step prevents one from failure.

（杨秀波 译）★★★★★●●

2. Discretion from beginning to end ensures success.

（王昌玲 译1）●●●●●

3. He who holds on to the very end would always achieve success.

（冯雷 译）★★★●●

4. Prudence all the way, success isn't far anyway.

（王绍昌 译）●●●●●

5. Success favors him who is prudent.

（王昌玲 译2）●●●●

6. If you can be as cautious at the end of doing a thing as you are at the beginning, you will never fail.

（杨中仁 译）★★●

7. No imprudence, no failure.

（铁冰 译）●●●

8. Where there is consistency, there is no failure but success.

（赵宜忠 译）★★

9. Anything can be done if one makes effort from the beginning to the end.

(李开林 译) ★

【16】合抱之木，生于毫末；九层之台，起于累土。

——《道德经·第六十四章》

投票：外方评委5人投票★，中方评委9人投票●

1. A giant tree grows from a tiny seedling；a towering platform rises from piled-up earth.

(丁如伟 译) ● ● ● ● ● ● ● ●

2. Giant trees grow out of tender seedlings；a high terrace is built with baskets of clay.

(樊功生 译) ★ ● ● ● ● ● ●

3. A small seed can grow into a big tree；collecting lumps of clay may build a high tower.

(彭智鹏 译) ★ ★ ★ ★

4. A tall tree grows from a hair-like blade；a high terrace starts with a small earthen base.

(冯雷 译) ● ● ● ●

5. A big tree comes from a tiny shoot，and a high platform from a dust.

(杨秀波 译) ● ● ● ●

6. A great oak grows from a little acorn. A high terrace rises from its very base.

(王成杰 译) ● ● ●

7. A towering thick tree buds from a tiny seed; a high terrace is piled up from the groundsill.

（王昌玲 译）●●●

8. Towering trees spring from tiny saplings; nine-story terraces start from piled soils.

（王绍昌 译）●●●

9. A tree as big as of two arms' hug started from something nearly unseen. A standing platform of nine stories is erected from earth within.

（郑晓春 译）★

【17】天地不仁，以万物为刍狗。——《道德经·第五章》

投票：外方评委8人投票★，中方评委4人投票●

1. Heaven and earth treat all beings alike.

（陈金金 译）★★★★★★★●●●

2. Nature shows no favoritism toward any living creature.

（王昌玲 译）★★★★★★●

3. The heaven and the earth have no moral judgement. All creatures are e-qual in their eyes.

（艾朝阳 译）★●●

4. Neither merciful nor merciless, the heaven and earth leave everything as it is.

（曹小菁 译）★●●

5. The universe is not benevolent to any particular thing. The universe is just a combination of everything's movement.

（孙玲玲 译）★●

6. The Heaven and Earth are no intentional Makers; everything in between only follows their own courses.

（石爱伟 译） ●●

7. Being fair and square is the way of the world.

（叶步青 译） ●●

8. Heaven and earth know no benevolence and see humans but the same as dogs, for they view all beings equal.

（石永浩 译） ●●

9. The universe favors none—it neither causes grass to grow for animals, nor breeds dogs for men.

（吴春晓 译） ★

【18】有无相生，难易相成。——《道德经·第二章》

投票：外方评委9人投票★，中方评委5人投票●

1. Things in nature coexist and correlate, such as nothing in relation to something and simplicity to difficulty.

（王梅兰 译） ★★★●●

2. Opposing states are always interdependent.

（冯雷 译） ★★★★

3. "Being" and "non-being", "difficult" and "easy" are relative and interdependent. Nothing exists all by itself.

（王昌玲 译） ★★●

4. Things and their opposites always come in pairs, such as being and non-being, difficult and easy.

（王成杰 译） ★●●

5. Taoism sees the world in interdependent binary oppositions, for example, presence and absence, and difficulty and easiness.

（吴春晓 译）★ ●

6. Being and non-being as well as ease and unease are integrated and interdependent.

（艾朝阳 译）★ ●

7. Possession and loss go hand in hand; difficulty and simplicity lie side by side.

（崔传明 译）★ ●

8. Opposite sides depend on each other.

（杨秀波 译）★ ●

9. Two things of opposite nature complement each other.

（魏红霞 译）★ ★

10. Being and non-being beget each other; difficulty and easiness complement each other.

（王毅 译）● ●

11. Qualities opposite presuppose each other, such as being and non-being, difficult and easy.

（石永浩 译）★

12. Existence and nonexistence generate each other; easiness and difficulty complement each other.

（董秀静 译）★

【19】 天之道，损有余而补不足。人之道则不然，损不足以奉有余。

——《道德经·第七十七章》

投票：外方评委 5 人投票★，中方评委 3 人投票●

1. While nature makes up for less with more, humans do the opposite.

（王成杰 译）★★★★

2. The way of Heaven is based on the balance between everything, but the way of the human being is different, which makes the poor poorer and the rich richer.

（张晓阳 译）★●●

3. The law of nature is to compensate the insufficient by reducing from the superabundant; but the law of human is different, which is often to contribute to the superabundant by grabbing from the insufficient.

（杨中仁 译）★●●

4. Nature is governed by the principle of equality, while man, the principle of equity.

（吴春晓 译）★●

5. The Way of Heaven reduces surpluses and replenishes scarcities; the Way of Human, on the contrary, reduces scarcities and replenishes surpluses.

（王绍昌 译）★●

6. The law of nature is to make up for scarcity by reducing surplus, while the law of men is to boost surplus by reducing scarcity.

（马建军 译）★●

7. In the natural world, surplus is taken to cover the shortages whereas in the human world, the rich always exploit the poor.

（冯雷 译）●●

名言警句英译

8. Nature always reduces the abundance to supplement the deficiencies. On the contrary, Society always impoverishes the poor to enrich the rich.

（王梅兰 译）★

9. Heaven balances the surplus and the shortage, but human beings do not.

（杨秀波 译）★

10. Nature robs the sufficient to help the deficient whereas man does the opposite.

（王昌玲 译）★

11. There must be a balance between the shortage and the remaining.

（任诚刚 译）★

12. The way of Heaven is to take the excessive to make up for the inadequate. The way of humanity is quite the opposite: the inadequate is still reduced to serve to the excessive.

（何冰 译）★

13. The law of nature is to reduce the resources of redundant ones to supplement the insufficient ones while the law of the society is just the opposite.

（董秀静 译）★

14. The Way of heaven is to diminish surplus and compensate for shortage; the Way of man is to impoverish the have-nots and enrich the haves.

（何艳 译）★

【20】天下难事，必作于易；天下大事，必作于细。

——《道德经·第六十三章》

投票：外方评委6人投票★，中方评委4人投票●

1. To do something big, you must start with something small.

(瑞雪 译) ★★★★★●

2. The difficult things under heaven evolve from easy ones, and the big things from small ones.

(何艳 译) ★●●

3. Difficult projects start from easy steps, large endeavors begin with small details.

(叶如钢 译) ●●

4. Difficulty grows from simplicity; significance lies in triviality.

(冯雷 译) ●●

5. All hard nuts grow from the soft ones, and all great things start from the little ones.

(张晓阳 译) ●

6. Difficulty starts with ease; greatness grows from detail.

(王成杰 译) ●

7. Step by step, even the most difficult thing can be done. Little by little, small events snowball into big ones.

(王昌玲 译) ●

8. Difficult tasks start from easy concepts; big deeds start from small details.

(孙玲玲 译) ●

9. To tackle the difficult, one should start with the easy. To accomplish something big, one should start with the trivial.

(王毅 译) ●

名言警句英译

10. Start from easy for the difficult, and pay attention to details for big affairs.

（樊功生 译）●

11. Many a little makes a mickle, and many a mickle makes a miracle.

（崔传明 译）●

【21】道生一，一生二，二生三，三生万物。

——《道德经·第四十二章》

投票：外方评委8人投票★，中方评委5人投票●

1. One gives birth to two, two gives birth to three, and three, to all living species.

（王昌玲 译）★★★●●

2. Every cause has its effect.

（崔传明 译）★★★★★

3. One begets two, two begets three and three begets the multitude.

（吴春晓 译）●●●

4. Tao begets one(universe), one begets two(Yin and Yang), two begets three(Heaven, Earth and Man), and three begets all things.

（张晓阳 译）●●●

5. Tao creates one, one creates two, two creates three, and three creates all things.

（何艳 译）★★

6. The Tao is the origin of one universe. The universe gives rise to two forces, Yin and Yang, which interact to generate a new being, the third being. Then all beings are created successively.

（马建军 译）●●

7. The way of Dao fathers one; from one comes two; from two comes three; from three comes the whole creation.

（乐国斌 译）●●

8. Dao begets one, one begets two, two begets three, and three begets multitudes.

（王绍昌 译）●●

9. Tao is unique. Tao itself contains Yin and Yang. The two intersect and form a well-balanced state. In this state, all things come into being.

（董秀静 译）●●

10. Out of Tao, One was born. Out of One, Two were formed. Out of Two, Three were made. Out of Three, all things were then created.

（叶如钢 译）★

【22】知足不辱，知止不殆。——《道德经·第四十四章》

投票：外方评委4人投票★，中方评委2人投票●

1. The one who is content will not be shamed, and the one who knows when to stop will not be harmed.

（樊功生 译）★★★●

2. Greed invites humiliation; moderation wards off danger.

（乐国斌 译）★★●

3. Contentment prevents humiliation, moderation prevents danger.

（何艳 译）★★●

4. Feeling content, you are away from humiliation; knowing when to stop, you are away from danger.

（王慧玉 译）★●

5. Greediness incurs disgrace, excessiveness invites risk.

（刘群 译）★★

6. Contentment keeps one free from possible shame and temperance keeps one safe from potential danger.

（董秀静 译）★

7. Avarice invites shame; moderation brings fame.

（石永浩 译）★

8. Satisfaction and self-restraint protect one from humiliation and dangers.

（曹小菁 译）★

9. Contentment avoids ignominy; moderation averts jeopardy.

（张俊锋 译）★

【23】致虚极，守静笃。万物并作，吾以观其复。

——《道德经·第十六章》

投票：外方评委4人投票★，中方评委2人投票●

1. Keep an empty and peaceful mind so you can see clearly how the universe evolves.

（王慧玉 译）★★●●

2. Do your best to cultivate your self to be empty-minded and keep fast in peace. When all things grow, I see them return to their origins.

（郁序新 译）★★●

3. My mind emptied, I stay in tranquility. Observing how things grow, I understand the cycle of life.

（石永浩 译）★★●

4. Clearing out all my thoughts and desires and attaining peace of mind, I watch all things grow and flourish to seek the truth.

(马建军 译) ★ ★

5. Clear your mind and stay composed. All living creatures are burgeoning together, which shows me the circle of life.

(伍敏毓 译) ★

6. Only by emptying our mind and calming our heart can we observe how the world repeats itself and learn the law of nature.

(冯雷 译) ★

7. I clean up my mind and keep it serene so as to understand the laws of nature.

(王成杰 译) ●

8. Let the soul attain its vacuous apex. Let the mind retain its ultimate peace. Myriads of matters undergo birth and decease. I thereby watch their regress.

(王绍昌 译1) ●

9. Evacuate thoughts in souls. Set mind in peace. Thousands of things bloom. I await their doom.

(王绍昌 译2) ●

10. Once you empty yourself of everything and keep yourself in an extremely still state, you'll be clear about the circulation laws of nature by observing all things alike go through their processes of activities.

(张晓阳 译) ●

【24】知者乐水，仁者乐山。——《论语·雍也》

投票：外方评委9人投票★，中方评委10人投票●

1. The wise love rivers and the kind love mountains.

（艾朝阳 译）★ ★ ● ● ● ● ● ●

2. The wise enjoy the flexibility of the flowing river, while the benevolent rejoice at the peace of the standing mountain.

（李开林 译）★ ★ ★ ● ● ●

3. The wise enjoy water for its agility and flexibility, while the humane enjoy mountains for their firmness and humanity.

（张俊锋 译）● ● ● ● ● ●

4. The wise are flexible as water whereas the benevolent are solid like mountains.

（王昌玲 译）★ ● ● ● ●

5. Man of knowledge enjoys water, man of kindness enjoys mountains.

（叶如钢 译）★ ★ ● ●

6. The wise love water; the benevolent love mountains.

（王绍昌 译）★ ★ ● ●

7. The love of the wise is as flexible as water; the love of the kind is as solid as a rock.

（王勋 译）★ ★ ●

8. The wit takes delight the way water runs along so merrily; the benevolent takes delight the way the mountain sits stably.

（程永生 译）★ ● ●

9. Waters enchant the wise whereas mountains delight the kind.

（乐国斌 译）★ ★ ★

10. The wise take delight in water, while the benevolent take delight in mountains.

（倪庆行 译）●●●

11. The joy of the wise is as clear as water crystal, and that of the benevolent is as high as the mountain unmovable.

（任诚刚 译）●●

12. The wise are intelligent as water, the benevolent steadfast as the mountain.

（张琼 译）●●

【25】三人行，必有我师焉；择其善者而从之，其不善者而改之。

——《论语·述而》

投票：外方评委3人投票★，中方评委10人投票●

1. Every dog has its day, all stars shine in their way; choose the superior to follow along and the inferior to right the wrong.

（冯雷 译）●●●●●●●

2. Among a company of three, there must be a teacher for me in one aspect or another. As for his merits, just follow suit; as for his demerits, correct them.

（倪庆行 译）★●●●●●

3. Every companion can be my teacher, as I can follow their merits and avoid their demerits.

（艾朝阳 译）●●●●●●

4. All can be my teachers; learn their merits but rectify their demerits.

（乐国斌 译）●●●●●

5. There is always a teacher for me in a company of three; their merits, I shall learn; their demerits, I shall spurn.

（张琼 译）●●●●●

6. There must be something I can learn from others, so I try to absorb the excellence they shine with to improve myself. Meanwhile, I keep alert to the disadvantages they may own and polish them immediately if I myself likewise have.

（李开林 译）★●●●

7. If I am with a tiger, a cat and a mouse, then they all can teach me something, be it a skill or a philosophical principle. I will learn shrewdness from the cat, pride from the tiger and diligence from the mouse. But I will not follow the cat to steal chickens or sleep the whole afternoon, the mouse to steal cheese and bite clothes, or the tiger to eat cows or even people.

（叶如钢 译）★★

8. Even in the company of three, at least one can teach me. I will emulate his merits and reflect whether I may have his possible demerits. If I do, I'll try to rectify them.

（王昌玲 译）★●

9. Among three people there must be one as my teacher. I'd choose their merits to learn, and see the shortcomings and reflect on myself, and make some corrections if there is any.

（任诚刚 译）★●

10. More often than not, I can learn from anyone, whose merits I learn and demerits I unlearn.

（石永浩 译）★●

11. Among three of us, the other two must be both teachers of mine. I learn the merits from the one and the other one's demerits I decline.

(赵宜忠 译) ●●

12. There is always something worth learning: good examples we follow, and bad examples we draw lessons from.

(曹小菁 译) ●●

【26】吾日三省吾身：为人谋而不忠乎？与朋友交而不信乎？传不习乎？

——《论语·学而》

投票：外方评委4人投票★，中方评委5人投票●

1. Each day I self reflect thrice: did I go all out to help others? Was I honest and sincere to my friends? Did I practice what was taught to me?

(王昌玲 译) ★★●●

2. I conduct daily retrospection with three questions: did I devote myself fully? Did I betray my friends? Did I practice what I preached?

(艾朝阳 译) ★★●

3. I reflect on three things daily: have I remained loyal to my team? Have I been honest to my friends? Have I reviewed and practised what my teacher taught me?

(冯雷 译1) ●●●

4. Daily reflections: am I an honest adviser? Am I a trustworthy friend? Am I a diligent student?

(冯雷 译2) ●●●

5. I examine myself on three things daily: am I devoted to my services? Am I committed to my friends? Am I engaged in studying my teacher's teachings?

（叶如钢 译）★ ●

6. Introspection into three questions is my routine assignment. Have I been unfaithful in counseling others? Have I been insincere to my friends? Have I failed to review what has been taught?

（倪庆行 译）● ●

7. Three times a day I reflect upon myself: do I serve with elaboration? Am I a man of integrity to my friends? Do I recapitulate what my teachers taught?

（刘群 译）● ●

8. My self-inspection goes everyday with three questions: have I worked dutifully? Have I befriended others truthfully? Have I learned exercisefully?

（铁冰 译）★

9. Every day I reflect on three points: have I been an honest counsellor? Have I been a faithful friend? Have I been a doer of what I teach?

（乐国斌 译）★

【27】君子和而不同，小人同而不和。——《论语·子路》

投票：外方评委 2 人投票★，中方评委 5 人投票●

1. Gentlemen respect each other though they may disagree. Mean men disgrace each other though they often agree.

（艾朝阳 译）★ ● ●

2. Gentlemen cherish harmony in diversity; villains seek unity without harmony.

（王绍昌 译1）★ ● ●

3. Gentlemen get on with each other but hold their own opinions; villains chime in with each other but have their own intentions.

（魏红霞 译）★ ●

4. Noble men differ in harmony; petty men discord in uniformity.

（曹小菁 译）● ●

5. The nobles value harmony but not uniformity; the villains targets uniformity but not harmony.

（王绍昌 译2）● ●

6. Great minds may differ in opinion but share the same heart; small minds appear to agree but their souls are far apart.

（冯雷 译）● ●

7. Gentlemen agree to disagree; petty men agree yet disagree.

（王昌玲 译）★

8. Without uniformity, decent people are still in harmony; with uniformity, despicable people still lack harmony.

（许霖越 译）★

【28】学而不思则罔，思而不学则殆。——《论语·为政》

投票：外方评委 8 人投票★，中方评委 6 人投票●

1. Learning without thinking makes no progress, and thinking without learning bears no fruit.

（冯雷 译1）★★★★★ ●

2. All study and no thinking makes one no gain in sight, all thinking and no study makes one risky in plight.

(赵宜忠 译) ●●●●●

3. Learning and thinking should go hand in hand, otherwise, you will end up confused or misled.

(王昌玲 译) ★★★●

4. Reading without thinking leads to confusion. Thinking without reading leads to deviation.

(张晔 译) ★●●●

5. To learn without thinking makes dull; to think without learning makes null.

(郁序新 译) ●●●●

6. All train and pain with no brain won't gain; all brain with no train and pain will be in vain.

(冯雷 译2) ★●●

7. One may get lost from studying without digesting, and will be ruined from musing without learning.

(樊功生 译) ●●●

8. All study and no thinking puts a student at a loss; all thinking and no study brings a student woes.

(乐国斌 译) ★★

9. Learners unthinking will remain confused; thinkers unlearning will be fruitless.

(铁冰 译) ●●

10. Superficial reading leads you astray; whimsical thinking leads you no-where.

(石永浩 译) ★

【29】言必信，行必果。——《论语·子路》

投票：外方评委6人投票★，中方评委5人投票●

1. Do what you say；finish what you do.

（冯雷 译1）★★★●●●

2. Promises must be kept and actions must be resolute.

（倪庆行 译）●●●●

3. Be truthful in what you say，be thorough in what you do.

（叶如钢 译1）★●●

4. Do what you say，achieve from what you do.

（任诚刚 译）★★★

5. Mean what you say，act without delay.

（魏红霞 译）●●●

6. Talk the talk，walk the walk.

（樊功生 译）★●

7. Attend to the promise；see to the result.

（王绍昌 译）★●

8. Break no promise；leave no job incomplete.

（刘群 译）★●

9. Be a man of your word. Carry it through，no matter what.

（王昌玲 译）★★

10. Keep your word；carry your actions through.

（叶如钢 译2）●●

11. Never eat your word；always complete your deed.

（曹小菁 译）●●

12. Keep your word and finish your work.

（彭智鹏 译1）★

13. Honor your promise and fulfill it.

（石永浩 译）★

14. Eat no words, and drink no actions.

（艾朝阳 译1）★

15. You can't unsay what you said; or undo what you have done.

（艾朝阳 译2）★

16. Always prove your words with your action, and further prove your action with firm resolution.

（杨秀波 译）★

17. Keep faithful to your word, and follow it through to the end.

（彭智鹏 译2）★

18. Don't just talk, act! Don't just start, finish!

（冯雷 译2）★

【30】其身正，不令而行；其身不正，虽令不从。

——《论语·子路》

投票：外方评委8人投票★，中方评委9人投票●

1. Men with integrity makes others follow them spontaneously, while others won't be able to do that even with force.

（张晔 译）★★★●●●●

2. Obedience is the reward for righteous conduct; disobedience is the cost of unprincipled behavior.

（冯雷 译）●●●●●●●

3. Leadership goes well with integrity but badly without it.

(石永浩 译) ★★★★★

4. If a leader is righteous, his policy will be performed; if iniquitous, it will be ignored despite his order.

(郁序新 译1) ●●●●●

5. As for administrators, if they are benevolent and exemplary, their orders will be obeyed; if not, their orders will be mere papers.

(石爱伟 译) ●●●●

6. Stand upright and then you'll walk straight without intending to; stand awry and then you'll walk lamed even with strength.

(艾朝阳 译1) ★★●

7. The example of righteous authority will be followed by people; of evil corruption, on the contrary, will be hated and rejected.

(郁序新 译2) ●●●

8. A self-disciplined official can have his policy carried out without giving orders, while an undisciplined one can't, even if he gives orders to enforce it.

(艾朝阳 译2) ●●●

9. A righteous official himself is a walking order; a corrupt official can order himself only.

(乐国斌 译) ●●

10. A leader of integrity will be followed with no order, but a devious one is disobeyed even with order.

(杨中仁 译) ★

11. A role model leads without talking. An empty talker leads none even with persuasion.

(王昌玲 译) ★

【31】 不在其位，不谋其政。——《论语·泰伯》

投票：外方评委9人投票★，中方评委10人投票●

1. If you hold not an office, you needn't interfere in other's duties.

　　　　　（郁序新 译1） ★★★★★★★

2. In position, in service. Out of position, out of service.

　　　　　（艾朝阳 译） ★★★★★

3. Mind your own business when it is none of your business.

　　　　　（杨中仁 译1） ★★★★●

4. Off the chair, off the affair.

　　　　　（郁序新 译2） ●●●●

5. Mind not how to drive if not sitting behind the wheel.

　　　　　（刘群 译） ★●●

6. Do whatever your position requires you to do, no more, no less!

　　　　　（王昌玲 译） ★★★

7. No power, no duty.

　　　　　（铁冰 译） ●●●

8. In public affairs, do what you should, not what you wish.

　　　　　（冯雷 译） ●●●

9. Out of power, out of affair.

　　　　　（张晓阳 译） ●●●

10. On the post, on duty; off the post, off duty.

　　　　　（陈赛花 译） ●●●

11. If not in charge, wield not the power.

　　　　　（石永浩 译） ★●

12. Don't dispose any affair in an office where you have no chair.

　　　　　（杨中仁 译2） ●●

13. He who takes charge knows his duty.

（赵宜忠 译）●●

14. Position held, duty bound.

（王绍昌 译）●●

15. Perform duty within its realm.

（王毅 译）●●

16. No position, no responsibility.

（樊功生 译）● ●

【32】君子成人之美，不成人之恶。——《论语·颜渊》

投票：外方评委6人投票★，中方评委5人投票●

1. A man of virtue would aid one in good deeds rather than abet one in evil things.

（丁如伟 译）★ ★ ● ● ●

2. An honorable man would help, not hurt others.

（董庆瑗 译）★ ★ ★ ★

3. A gentleman encourages good behavior and stops evil behavior.

（何艳 译）★ ★ ●

4. A real gentleman knows when to help and when to stand aloof.

（吴春晓 译）★ ● ●

5. A nobleman encourages one's benevolence but discourages one's malevolence.

（孙玲玲 译）★ ● ●

6. Altruism defines a gentleman, and egoism a crooked man.

（刘向军 译）★ ●

7. A man of virtue never facilitates an evil deed, but helps others to fulfil their good wishes.

（陈金金 译）★ ★

8. A gentleman helps a man fulfill his wishes, but encourages no evil in him.

（石爱伟 译）● ●

9. A gentleman does favour but never evil to others.

（杨中仁 译）● ●

10. A virtuous man helps one to achieve, but never incites one to misbe-have.

（魏红霞 译）● ●

11. A righteous man helps others in need, not in conducting an evil deed.

（曹小菁 译）● ●

【33】往者不可谏，来者犹可追。——《论语·微子》

投票：外方评委7人投票★，中方评委3人投票●

1. Let bygones be bygones! Focus on what comes.

（王昌玲 译）★ ★ ●

2. We cannot rewrite our past, but we can write our future.

（冯雷 译，改编自网上名言）★ ★ ★

3. While the past can't be retrieved, the upcoming is to be pursued.

（何艳 译）● ● ●

4. Let go of the past and look forward to the future.

（王毅 译）★★

5. The past is irreparable, while the future is shapable.

（倪庆行 译）●●

6. No more regret over the past failure! Seize the time to strive for a better future!

（刘向军 译）●●

7. Bygones are beyond rectifying or undoing—set your sights on what is coming.

（叶步青 译）●●

8. The past is irrevocable, but the future is not too late.

（任诚刚 译）★

9. The history in the past, the hope in the future.

（钱朝晖 译）★

10. The past is way beyond advising; the future can still be counseled.

（王绍昌 译）★

11. The past is the past, but the future can be changed.

（陶家乐 译）★

【34】后生可畏，焉知来者之不如今也。——《论语·子罕》

投票：外方评委8人投票★，中方评委7人投票●

1. Young generations have a lot of potential. Who knows they wouldn't surpass us?

（王梅兰 译）★●●●●●

2. Never laugh at the saplings! Someday they will amaze you with heights.

（石永浩 译）★●●●●●

3. Do not look down on young people.

（陶家乐 译）★★★★★

4. The potentials of the younger generation could never be underestimated. How do you know that they will not overtake us one day?

（冯雷 译）★●●●

5. Every oak has been an acorn, so successors outdo predecessors.

（王成杰 译，借用英语谚语）★●●

6. Next generation always rocks the world. You never know by how much they will exceed us today.

（李开林 译）★●●

7. To be young is to awe. How could we know that juniors are inferior to seniors?

（王婷 译）★●●

8. There is ample reason to fear the youth. How do you know they won't surpass the present?

（杨胜悦 译）★★

9. Young people have the potential, to be adored. How can we know that their future will not match the people of today?

（任诚刚 译）●●

10. Youths are to be regarded with respect. How do you know that they won't surpass us in time?

（马建军 译，部分借用词典）●●

11. The young are worthy of our respect and awe. How can you know the next generation is less than the present?

（王昌玲 译）★

12. Beware, the younger generation may yet be more than our equals.

（叶步青 译）★

【35】 当仁不让于师。——《论语·卫灵公》

投票：外方评委4人投票★，中方评委5人投票●

1. As to kindness and morality, you don't need to be after your mentor.

（王梅兰 译）★ ★ ● ●

2. My mentors are dear to me, but dearer still is truth.

（王成杰 译，改编自 Aristotle 名言）★ ● ●

3. Benevolence takes priority over teachers' authority.

（丁如伟 译）★ ●

4. To do the right thing is more important than to follow the teacher's instructions.

（孙玲玲 译）★ ●

5. When demonstrating empathy, the student does not need to follow his teacher.

（冯雷 译）★ ●

6. Charity knows no difference between teachers and students.

（石永浩 译）★ ●

7. Benevolence teaches best.

（曹小菁 译）★ ●

8. A moral man should follow the principle of benevolence and righteousness, no matter who he is, a student or a teacher.

（郁序新 译）● ●

9. Some things that you should do, should be done without hesitation.

（陶家乐 译）★

【36】 朝闻道，夕死可矣。——《论语·里仁》

投票：外方评委6人投票★，中方评委4人投票●

1. It is never too late to learn.

（吴春晓 译，借用英语谚语）★★★★★★

2. Enlightenment is all a life needs to be well lived.

（杨胜悦 译）★●●

3. Learn a good lesson and there will be no regret at the end of the day.

（何冰 译）★★★

4. Let me be enlightened with the Truth; then I fear not the pending death.

（张建惠 译）●●●

5. The Master said, "if I attain enlightenment in the morning, I will die content in the evening."

（王绍昌 译）●●●

6. Once enlightened in the morning, one may die content in the evening.

（倪庆行 译）●●

7. If I learned the Tao in the morning, I would die without regret in the evening.

（石爱伟 译）●●

8. He who knows the truth shall die without regret.

（王成杰 译）★

9. Truth is above everything, even death.

（孙玲玲 译）★

【37】博学而笃志，切问而近思。——《论语·子张》

投票：外方评委 5 人投票★，中方评委 3 人投票●

1. To be a scholar, one should be erudite, tenacious, inquisitive, and contemplative.

（王成杰 译）★★★●

2. Be dedicated and learn broadly. Be inquisitive and think critically.

（何冰 译）★●●●

3. Be learned and determined; be inquisitive and reflective.

（乐国斌 译）★★●

4. Strive to be erudite, attentive, inquisitive and reflective.

（王昌玲 译）★★★

5. Read extensively and stay focused; ask questions sincerely and think about current issues.

（何艳 译）★●

6. Learning involves extensive reading, constant pursuing, well-conducted questioning and reality-based practicing.

（吴春晓 译）●●

7. Learn broadly and stay determined; inquire sincerely and ponder the current matters.

（叶如钢 译）●●

8. Learn widely and stick to your goal; ask questions earnestly and reflect on things at hand.

（马建军 译）★

名言警句英译

【38】老者安之，朋友信之，少者怀之。——《论语·公冶长》

投票：外方评委7人投票★，中方评委4人投票●

1. Comfort the elderly, trust your friends, and take care of the youngsters.

（何冰 译）★★★★★★●

2. Let the elderly be blessed, friends be cherished, and the young be supported.

（王绍昌 译）★★●●

3. Comfort the aged, trust any friend and care about many a child.

（曹小菁 译）★★●

4. An ideal society is to have a secure environment for the elderly, an honest one for the adult and a caring one for children.

（张晔 译）★★●

5. Seniors supported, friends trusted, children nurtured.

（王成杰 译）★●●

6. May the elderly live in peace and the young under care. May friends and colleagues trust each other.

（吴春晓 译）★●

7. Let the old live a comfortable worry-free life. Let the young progress with love and care. Win the trust of my friends.

（王梅兰 译）★●

8. My aspiration is that the old can be settled, friends can be trusted and children can be cared.

（张立国 译）●●

9. My aspiration is to let the young be cared for, the elderly enjoy happiness, and friends trust each other.

（马建军 译）★

10. My ideal well-governed state is one in which the elderly enjoy a peaceful life, people trust one another like friends, and the young are adequately looked after.

（石爱伟 译）★

11. The old long for safety, the intimate for trust and the young for appreciation.

（丁后银 译）★

12. I aim to make the seniors comfortable, to entrust friends and endear the young.

（王昌玲 译）★

13. I hope the elderly enjoy peace, friends enjoy trust and children enjoy care.

（冯雷 译）★

【39】名不正，则言不顺；言不顺，则事不成。

——《论语·子路》

投票：外方评委10人投票★，中方评委4人投票●

1. If you have a proper title, your words will carry weight, and then you can get things done.

（王成杰 译）★★★★★★★★●

2. If your reputation is not established, your words are not accepted, and things are not accomplished.

（冯雷 译）★★★★★★

3. If there is no moral justification, what is said cannot be followed. Accordingly, nothing can be accomplished.

（马建军 译）★★●●

4. If a person's status and title is not recognized and justified, his words will not be considered reasonable. Neither will the things he desires be accomplished successfully.

（董秀静 译）★★★

5. If you're in the wrong position, your words won't make sense. If your words don't make sense, you can't accomplish anything.

（瑞雪 译）●●●

6. If the title is not right, the words will not carry weight, and things cannot be done.

（乐国斌 译）★●

7. Nothing could be done if not justified.

（吴春晓 译）●●

8. Without a proper name, you cannot justify your action. If you cannot justify your action, it will come to nothing.

（王昌玲 译）●●

【40】不义而富且贵，于我如浮云。——《论语·述而》

投票：外方评委7人投票★，中方评委4人投票●

1. Wealth and rank obtained in an unrighteous manner are nothing but floating clouds to me.

（石爱伟 译）★★●●●

2. Undeserved wealth and status are worthless for me, just like fleeting clouds.

（叶如钢 译）★ ★ ★ ●

3. Wealth and rank obtained by foul means are but floating clouds to me.

（王毅 译）★ ★ ● ●

4. Ill-gotten fame and wealth to me are no more than floating clouds.

（田璐 译）★ ★ ● ●

5. Things not earned by hard work of fortune have no meaning.

（陶家乐 译）★ ★

6. Unrighteous wealth and ranks are just sailing clouds to me.

（乐国斌 译）● ●

7. Wealth and honour acquired by unjustifiable means mean nothing to me, just like a cloud in the sky.

（董秀静 译）● ●

8. Wealth and rank without integrity are nothing but transient clouds to me.

（王如利 译）★

9. To profit through dishonest means is like floating aimlessly as a cloud; meaningless and without reward.

（杨胜悦 译）★

【41】慎终追远，民德归厚矣。——《论语·学而》

投票：外方评委7人投票★，中方评委4人投票●

1. Respect for ancestors makes a respectful and respectable nation.

（王慧玉 译）★ ★ ★ ★ ★ ●

2. When proper funerals for the elderly and sacrificial rites for ancestors become a tradition, virtue naturally prevails in the nation.

（石永浩 译）★★●●●

3. By treating the dead with respect and drawing lessons from the past, public morals will be cultivated.

（王如利 译）★★★★

4. Respectfully mourning the passing of parents and commemorating ancestors are sure to cultivate integrity and loyalty among the people.

（乐国斌 译）★★★★

5. If a king gives his parents proper burials and respect his ancestors, his subjects will follow suit and be virtuous.

（吴春晓 译）★●

6. Pay your respect to your late parents with a proper funeral, and your ancestors with memorials, so that good customs among the people and for the nation follow.

（刘群 译）★●

7. What a virtuous nation we will be, if all people honor life and try to emulate the sages of yore.

（王昌玲 译）★●

8. If people can be respectful to their parents who have passed away and always remember their ancestors, the folk customs will naturally become more and more honest.

（董秀静 译）★★

9. According to Zengzi, a representative figure of Confucianism, if a state can effectively guide its people to seriously perform funeral rites to their parents and sincerely hold sacrificial rites to their ancestors, the civic virtue can be gradually enhanced.

（王毅 译）●●

10. We should perform the proper funeral rites for the deceased and reverently honor our ancestors, so that the virtue of citizens will be promoted.

(马建军 译) ★

11. Thinking of good deeds of the deceased piously, and valuing the funerals of one's parents lead to people's heightened moral awareness and the custom of kindness.

(杨秀波 译) ★

【42】君子喻于义，小人喻于利。——《论语·里仁》

投票：外方评委 3 人投票★，中方评委 1 人投票●

1. A noble person is guided by moral principles, whereas a base person by his own gains.

(叶如钢 译) ★★★★

2. Gentlemen seek moral principles; petty men seek monetary gains.

(樊功生 译) ★★★

3. Men of virtue care about morality; petty men care about profitability.

(王昌玲 译) ★★

4. In decision making, a noble man prioritizes justice, while a mean man prioritizes personal gains.

(石永浩 译) ★★

5. The gentleman sees righteousness; the petty man sees profit.

(任诚刚 译) ★

6. People of integrity keep morality in mind, while the selfish ones only see benefit.

(王慧玉 译) ★

7. A gentleman understands other people's pain, but an unprincipled person only cares about personal gain.

（冯雷 译）★

8. A noble man is versed in righteousness, while a mean person is versed in gain.

（马建军 译）●

9. A noble heart values faith most; a snob only favors profits.

（董庆瑗 译）●

10. A great mind strives for justice, while a base one only cares about benefits.

（吴春晓 译）●

【43】夫战，勇气也；一鼓作气，再而衰，三而竭。

——左丘明《左传·庄公十年》

投票：外方评委5人投票★，中方评委6人投票●

1. War, an act of courage, is critical in its first strike. Success diminishes in subsequent strikes.

（樊功生 译）★ ★ ★ ★ ★ ●

2. Fighting is driven by courage, which is much at the first run, less at the second, and least at the third.

（曹小菁 译）● ● ● ●

3. To win is a matter of valor which is spurred by the first bout of drumbeating, dwindled by the second and exhausted by the third.

（倪庆行 译）● ● ●

4. Mettle matters most in war. At the first beating of the drum, the attacking side is spirited; at the second beating, dispirited; at the third beating, exhausted.

（乐国斌 译）●●●

5. At one go we will drive out the foe!

（郁序新 译）★●

6. At one go you must win, or your courage will wane.

（石永浩 译）★●

7. Battles are tests of courage. Go all out and strike to win. The strength wanes in a second strike and runs out in a third one.

（叶如钢 译）★★

8. To win a battle, one must fight with might. When the war drum beats first, he's bestirred most; second, weakened; third, exhausted.

（魏红霞 译）●●

9. Courage is crucial for winning a battle. First drum-beating charge is decisive, second is less powerful, third turns impotent.

（冯雷 译）●●

10. War is a matter of valor: the first beating of drums boosts the morale, the second beating diminishes it, and the third exhausts it.

（王昌玲 译）●●

【44】言之无文，行而不远。

——左丘明《左传·襄公二十五年》

投票：外方评委10人投票★，中方评委7人投票●

1. Words without taste won't last.

（樊功生 译）★★★●●●

2. Writing is an art, style is the heart. Without the heart, the art dies fast.

（冯雷 译）★ ★ ● ● ● ●

3. Elegance gives wings to writings.

（石永浩 译）★ ★ ★ ★ ●

4. With eloquence, writing takes wings.

（王昌玲 译1）★ ★ ★ ● ●

5. A finely-knitted text will be savored by a great number of readers.

（石爱伟 译）★ ★ ★ ★ ★

6. Speech without polish won't spread far and fast.

（魏红霞 译）● ● ● ● ●

7. Style and skill are the wings of words.

（叶如钢 译1）★ ● ● ●

8. Empty writings will not travel afar.

（倪庆行 译）★ ★ ★

9. Without art, literature won't last.

（杨秀波 译）★ ●

10. Truth poorly said is poorly spread.

（铁冰 译）★ ●

11. As far as speech is concerned, no eloquence, no effect.

（王昌玲 译2）★ ★

12. Well phrased work is far more compelling.

（李开林 译）★ ★

13. Words without rhetoric will not go popular.

（艾朝阳 译）● ●

14. Speech without rhetoric leaves no impression.

（杨中仁 译）● ●

15. Passages without polish won't be popular.

（王绍昌 译）● ●

16. Works in fine words last long.

（彭智鹏 译）●●

17. It takes style for anything written or spoken to become popular.

（叶如钢 译2）★

【45】多行不义必自毙。——左丘明《左传·隐公元年》

投票：外方评委6人投票★，中方评委6人投票●

1. "What goes around comes around."

（王梅兰 译，引用）★★★★●

2. A bad man will fall victim to his own conduct.

（冯雷 译）★●●

3. Evil doing backfires.

（石永浩 译）★●

4. Committing numerous injustices results in self-destruction.

（叶如钢 译）★●

5. Bad deeds bring downfall.

（杨胜悦 译）★●

6. Those who commit evil deeds will be condemned by the LORD sooner or later.

（王毅 译）★★

7. He is doomed to die who often practices evil.

（倪庆行 译）●●

8. Doomed are the incorrigible.

（刘向军 译）●●

9. Too many evil doings will inevitably lead one to self-destruction.

（史红霞 译）●●

10. Too much mischief is bound to ruin oneself.

（任诚刚 译）●●

11. Injustices lead to destruction.

（张立国 译）★

12. He that does evil shall find evil.

（马建军 译，借用英语谚语）★

13. He who does much wrong is doomed to self-destruction.

（马金龙 译）★

14. Unrestrained injustice must result in self-destruction.

（何艳 译）★

15. Much evil-doing leads to one's downfall.

（杨秀波 译）★

【46】民生在勤，勤则不匮。——左丘明《左传·宣公十二年》

投票：外方评委7人投票★，中方评委5人投票●

1. Industry is the key to avoidance of deficiency.

（石爱伟 译）★★●●

2. Diligence prevents indigence.

（孙玲玲 译）★★●●

3. Diligence produces affluence.

（王梅兰 译）★●●●

4. Industry rewards people with an affluent life.

(王昌玲 译) ★ ★ ●

5. Diligence is the basis of a decent living.

(何艳 译) ★ ★ ●

6. To live well, work hard. Industry drives away poverty.

(王成杰 译) ★ ●

7. The livelihood of the people lies in hard work, and hard work brings affluence.

(史红霞 译) ★ ●

8. A good life lies in diligence, which promises opulence.

(张俊锋 译) ● ●

9. People's livelihood depends on diligence and diligent people will not be short of means of livelihood.

(董秀静 译) ● ●

10. Industrious people thrive.

(何冰 译) ★

11. A good life consists in diligence which brings affluence.

(马建军 译) ★

12. Hard work allows for an abundance of essentials.

(陶家乐 译) ★

13. Diligence boosts production and improves livelihoods.

(冯雷 译) ★

14. Life centres around diligence, and diligence resists loss.

(杨胜悦 译) ★

【47】度德而处之，量力而行之。

——左丘明《左传·隐公十一年》

投票：外方评委9人投票★，中方评委4人投票●

1. Do things in accordance with your moral principles and capabilities.

（石永浩 译）★★★★★★★★★●

2. Base your behavior on your morals, and act within the limits of your ability.

（叶如钢 译）★★★★★●●●

3. Conduct yourself according to moral standards, take action according to your ability.

（何艳 译）★★★★★●●●

4. We should weigh our own virtue when dealing with other people and evaluate our own ability when doing things.

（董秀静 译）★★★★★

5. Act on the basis of morality and competence.

（王成杰 译）★★●●

6. Conduct yourself according to virtue; accomplish things according to ability.

（王昌玲 译）★●●●

7. Behave yourself with good virtue and conduct well with your ability.

（郁序新 译）★●●

8. Be who you are and do what you can.

（王如利 译）★●

9. Handle affairs according to normal standards and one's practical ability.

（张晓阳 译）★●

10. Behave in line with your virtue and ability.

（倪庆行 译）★★

11. Do what you can with what you have.

（陶家乐 译）★★

12. Conduct in accordance with virtue and do what within capacity.

（王毅 译）●●

13. Act according to your moral strength and capabilities.

（马建军 译）★

14. Be sure of your own virtue when dealing with people, and be aware of your own strength before initiating a plan.

（吴春晓 译）★

【48】兵无常势，水无常形。——孙武《孙子兵法·虚实》

投票：外方评委16人投票★，中方评委16人投票●

1. No form for water; no norm for war.

（曹小菁 译）★★★★●●●●●●●●

2. There is only one constant in water and warfare: change.

（王绍昌 译1）★★★★★★★●

3. Just as water takes no fixed form, the art of war lies in strategy flexible.

（王昌玲 译1）●●●●●●●●

4. Water changes its way in accord with the terrain; so does war strategy in accord with the enemy.

（李红雨 译）★★★★●●

5. The art of war changes with the condition. The shape of water depends on its container.

(孟朝岗 译) ★★●●●●

6. Warfare has no permanent momentum just as water has no permanent shape.

(倪庆行 译1) ★●●●●●

7. There is no fixed strategy in war, just as water has no constant shape.

(王琳 译) ★★★●●

8. Warfare has no fixed strategy just as water has no fixed shape.

(华卫 译1) ★★★●●

9. The art of war is adjust to ever-changing circumstances, the nature of water is adapt to ever-changing conditions.

(冯雷 译) ★●●●

10. Formless water mirrors the art of war.

(王昌玲 译2) ●●●●

11. Water assumes no constancy, as warfare displays no permanency.

(王绍昌 译2) ●●●●

12. Warfare defies the norm. Water takes any form.

(陈良 译) ●●●●

13. Tactics is to army what form is to water.

(于元元 译) ●●●●

14. Water has shapes galore, so does the art of war.

(倪庆行 译2) ★●●

15. Water and war share intangible forms.

(艾朝阳 译) ★●

16. The warfare is as flexible as the water.

(彭智鹏 译) ●●

17. Constant changes lie in the strategy of war as well as in the shape of water.

（华卫 译2）●●

【49】上下同欲者胜，风雨同舟者兴。

——语本孙武《孙子兵法·谋攻》："上下同欲者胜。"

投票：外方评委5人投票★，中方评委8人投票●

1. To win a battle, both general and soldiers must fight for the same goal; to achieve prosperity, all must stand through wind and rain as a whole.

（冯雷 译1）★★★★●●●●●

2. If those at different levels are of the same mind, they will prevail; if those in the same boat share weal and woe, they will prosper.

（倪庆行 译1）★★●●●

3. Armies of one mind triumph, companies of one will thrive.

（乐国斌 译）●●●●●

4. A team having a common goal will triumph; a group striving together will thrive.

（铁冰 译）★★●

5. Mind-sharers lead; journey-farers win.

（王绍昌 译）●●●

6. If all ranks want to fight, a troop prevails. If all stick together through storms, a team thrives.

（叶如钢 译）●●●

7. Mutual desires from different rankings will lead to triumph; solidarity to weather storms in the same boat will result in prosperity.

（倪庆行 译2）●

8. When the general and soldiers are one hearted, they shall win. When people are in the same boat, rain or sunshine, they shall survive to thrive.

（王昌玲 译）●

9. Nothing is impossible for those of one mind and in the same boat.

（冯雷 译2）●

10. Think together and suffer together, then you will overcome.

（艾朝阳 译）●

【50】是故百战百胜，非善之善者也；不战而屈人之兵，善之善者也。

——孙武《孙子兵法·谋攻》

投票：外方评委2人投票★，中方评委4人投票●

1. To win without battle shows the supreme military art.

（郁序新 译）●●●●

2. To win by fighting, although successful each time, is not ideal. To conquer without a fight is nonetheless the ultimate.

（樊功生 译）●●●

3. Winning all battles through fighting is not the best strategy at all; defeating the enemy without having to fight is the full reward of all.

（冯雷 译）●●●

4. Hence to fight and be ever victorious is not the top tactic at all. The supreme strategist forces the enemy to withdraw without a battle.

（王绍昌 译）★●

5. Hence, to fight and win all battles is not of the highest caliber. Of the highest caliber is to subdue the enemy with no battle.

（叶如钢 译）●●

6. Thus it isn't the best to win in a hundred battles big or small, but to defeat the enemy with no battle is the best of all.

（赵宜忠 译）●●

7. The best warrior is not to win in every fight but to win without resorting to fight.

（艾朝阳 译）●●

8. Therefore, winning tactfully, instead of winning frequently, is the best way to win.

（曹小菁 译1）●

9. Therefore, victory in each battle is not virtuous, for it still involves killing. The most virtuous victory is to crush your enemies without killing.

（王昌玲 译）●

10. By contrast, winning a hundred wars is not so rewarding, winning without a war is the most rewarding.

（曹小菁 译2）●

【51】静如处子，动如脱兔。

——语本孙武《孙子兵法·九地》："始如处女，敌人开户；后如脱兔，敌不及拒。"

投票：外方评委9人投票★，中方评委5人投票●

1. An army shall be quick and nimble when it moves, and be silent and still when stationed.

（孙壮 译）★★★★★★★★★

2. When in preparation, be as silent as a rock; when in action, be as nimble as a hare.

（王成杰 译）★●●●

3. An army should keep as still and quiet as a virgin, and move as agile and fast as a rabbit.

（孙玲玲 译）★★●

4. A strategist knows when and how to launch a surprise attack.

（刘向军 译）●●●

5. Being flexible between composure and promptness is the key to winning a battle.

（张莹 译）★●

6. Still as a virgin, speedy as a hare.

（崔传明 译）●●

7. In military operations, be restrained as a virgin or swift as a hare as needed.

（冯雷 译）●●

8. Stay poised as a graceful virgin and act swift as a leopard.

（王毅 译）★

9. The temperament of a soldier is like this: standing still as a pillar, moving fast as a hare.

(郁序新 译) ★

10. Be still as a pool of water before the battle; be swift as a streak of lightning during the strike.

(叶步青 译) ★

名言警句英译

【52】用师者王，用友者霸，用徒者亡。——《曾子》

投票：外方评委6人投票★，中方评委2人投票●

1. Modesty helps to rule a country, friendliness benefits a team, but favoritism would only lead to failure.

(吴春晓 译) ★ ★ ★ ★ ★

2. Rulers tutored by masters excel; rulers assisted by friends swell; rulers accompanied by flatterers fail.

(王绍昌 译) ★ ★ ● ●

3. Modesty enables you to realize your aspiration. Sincerity assists you in boosting your occupation. Vanity keeps you from reaching your expectation.

(伍敏毓 译) ★ ● ●

4. Under the guidance of a teacher one can become a king, with the help of friends one can be an overlord, and one will perish when relying on idlers.

(叶如钢 译) ★ ●

5. One who treats talents as teachers wins the whole world; one who treats talents as friends wins a state; one who treats talents as slaves is doomed to failure.

(王毅 译) ★ ●

6. Among all the warring states he who treats his helpers like mentors will become king; he who treats his subordinates like friends will become a strong reginal ruler; he who uses sweet-mouthed but incompetent officials will be annihilated.

（石爱伟 译） ★

7. For a ruler, he'll become emperor if choosing his teachers to assist himself, king if choosing his friends, and a failure if choosing yes-men.

（马建军 译） ★

8. A leader who treats the wise men as teachers and friends will succeed, while a leader who treats the wise men as servants will fail.

（何艳 译） ★

【53】为者常成，行者常至。——《晏子春秋·内篇杂下》

投票：外方评委17人投票★，中方评委15人投票●

1. Keep working, you will achieve; keep walking, you will arrive.

（孟朝岗 译） ★★★★★★★★★★★●●●●●●

2. Keep doing and you may succeed; keep going and you will proceed.

（石永浩 译） ★★★●●●●●●●●●●●●●●

3. Those who keep doing will achieve; those who keep going will arrive.

（许霖越 译） ★★★★★★★★●●●●●●

4. Perseverance is always the best policy for work or travel.

（冯雷 译1） ★★★★★★★★

5. Walk on and on and you will arrive; work on and on and you will achieve.

（王国己 译） ★★★★★★★★

6. Whatever you do, do it sound and hard; wherever you go, go with soul and heart.

(冯雷 译2) ★★★●●●

7. Never give up and you'll succeed anyway.

(艾朝阳 译) ★★★★★●

8. Perseverance and persistence, elements of success.

(杨晓斌 译) ★★★●

9. The doer succeeds; the traveler arrives.

(王绍昌 译1) ★★●●

10. Never quit, and you will make it.

(倪庆行 译1) ★★●

11. A determined doer succeeds often; a tireless traveler surely reaches the destination.

(李红雨 译) ★★★

12. In doing and going, we arrive and achieve.

(王绍昌 译2) ●●●

13. Doing promises achieving, going promises arriving.

(程永生 译) ●●●

14. First be a doer, and you shall be an achiever, sooner or later.

(王昌玲 译) ★●

15. He who acts unceasingly, always accomplishes, and he who constantly moves forward, always arrives.

(欧永福 译) ★★

16. Unceasing action always achieves a feat, while constant plodding always has a destination to greet.

(倪庆行 译2) ●●

【54】 老吾老以及人之老，幼吾幼以及人之幼。

——《孟子·梁惠王上》

投票：外方评委 14 人投票★，中方评委 15 人投票●

1. My love and care for the old and young start from my family and extend to the others.

（艾朝阳 译）★★★★★★★★●●●●●

2. Respect your parents and also the parents of others；love your children and also the children of others.

（李红雨 译）★★★★★★●●●●●●

3. Honour your parents and extend this honour to the parents of others；care for your children and extend this care for the children of others.

（冯雷 译1）★●●●●●

4. We should respect the old and love the young of others as we do our own.

（程永生 译）●●●●●●

5. One should treat parents and children of others as if they are his own.

（许霖越 译）★★★★★

6. Respect the aged in other families in the same way you respect the aged in your own family；love children in other families in the same way you love your own children.

（倪庆行 译）●●●●●

7. I respect the old as I would my parents；I care the young as I would my children.

（王琳 译）●●●●●

8. I respect all seniors，and protect all minors as my own flesh and blood.

（王昌玲 译）●●●●

9. Don't forget other parents while supporting your own. Don't forget other children while raising your own.

（任诚刚 译）●●●●

10. Respect thy parents and care for thy children; for those of others thy love shall not lessen.

（冯雷 译2）●●●

11. We should love and support the old as we would our parents and the young as we would our children.

（刘群 译）★●

12. Take filial care of my family elders as well as others', care for our own children affectionately as well as others'.

（陆峰 译）●●

【55】天时不如地利，地利不如人和。

——《孟子·公孙丑下》

投票：外方评委3人投票★，中方评委9人投票●

1. Victory in war depends more on well-integrated human strength than on topographical advantages, and more on topographical advantages than on time-favored opportunities.

（铁冰 译）★★●●●

2. Heaven's favorable weather is inferior to earth's advantageous terrain, which is in turn inferior to human unity.

（倪庆行 译）●●●●

3. The right time is no better than the right place and the right place is no better than the harmony of man.

（任诚刚 译） ●●●

4. As far as importance is concerned, harmony outshines location which outshines timing.

（王昌玲 译1） ●●●

5. Which plays an important role in a battle timing is next to geolocation, which in turn next to inner unity.

（魏红霞 译） ●●●

6. The right time, favorable position, harmonious human environment are in hierarchical order of importance.

（石永浩 译1） ●●●

7. Heaven-sent opportunity helps; favored situation matters; human unison works.

（冯雷 译1） ●●●

8. Right timing is important, but more so are location and topographic advantages, and even more important are harmony and unity of people.

（叶如钢 译） ★●

9. To win the battle, opportunity is heaven sent, favored condition is crucial, and human support is essential.

（冯雷 译2） ★●

10. The right place is more important than the right time, but less important than the right persons.

（石永浩 译2） ●●

11. Among the three advantages, harmony is the best, good location is the better, favorable time is good.

（杨秀波 译） ●●

12. Location is more important than timing;people harmony is more important than location.

（王绍昌 译）★

13. A good timing is less important than a strategic position,which is less valuable than joint effort.

（王昌玲 译2）★

【56】得道者多助，失道者寡助。——《孟子·公孙丑下》

投票：外方评委4人投票★，中方评委4人投票●

1. Those virtuous win many supporters;those vicious have few followers.

（曹小菁 译）★★★★●●

2. He who reigns with benevolence is well supported. He who reigns without benevolence shall be deserted.

（王昌玲 译1）★★●●●

3. The just are supported by many,the unjust are supported by few.

（叶如钢 译）★★●●

4. A just cause has many helpers,while an unjust one finds few followers.

（任诚刚 译）●●●

5. He who wins the hearts of all wins the world;he who loses the hearts of all loses the world.

（王昌玲 译2）●●●

6. People support the benign but combat the brutal.

（魏红霞 译）★★

7. A just man has more helpers old and new, but an unjust one has few.

（赵宜忠 译）●●

8. Those upholding justice will have sufficient support, while those not will find little.

（李开林 译）★

【57】人之患，在好为人师。——《孟子·离娄上》

投票：外方评委3人投票★，中方评委4人投票●

1. One weakness of human nature is his willingness to be others' teacher.

（冯雷 译1）★●●●

2. Being fond of sermonizing others is really a weakness.

（石永浩 译1）★●●

3. One human weakness lies in acting as the knowing-all teacher.

（石爱伟 译）●●●

4. Man's biggest vice is his readiness to give unsolicited advice.

（王昌玲 译）★●

5. It is a weakness of man to be too ready to act like a teacher to others if you are not one.

（石永浩 译2）●●

6. Readiness to teach others is human weakness.

（王绍昌 译）●●

7. The trouble of people is that they like to be others' teachers.

（任诚刚 译）★

8. A person's grave fault lies in his self-righteousness to believe he is entitled to teach even though he should be taught.

（杨秀波 译）★

9. People like to offer advice or give instructions without being asked, which is actually a human flaw.

（冯雷 译2）★

【58】穷则独善其身，达则兼济天下。

——《孟子·尽心上》

投票：外方评委9人投票★，中方评委11人投票●

1. When poor, cultivate and discipline yourself; when rich, contribute and distribute your wealth.

（王绍昌 译）★★★★★★★★●●

2. If you can, better the world; if you can't, better yourself.

（石永浩 译）★●●●●●●

3. Manage yourself in poverty; help others when wealthy.

（曹小菁 译）★★★●●

4. Pick up yourself in gloom; raise up the world in boom.

（郁序新 译）●●●●●

5. Uphold your integrity when in poverty and benefit the whole world when in prosperity.

（倪庆行 译）●●●●●

6. In adversity, help yourself; in prosperity, help others.

（王昌玲 译1）★★★★

7. When poor, be independent; when rich, be benevolent.

（魏红霞 译）★●●●

8. A gentleman sticks to self-cultivation if fate goes against him; he aims for the good of the world when fortune smiles upon him.

（石爱伟 译）★●●●

9. Being poor, earn your bread; being rich, share your bread.

（张琼 译）★●●

10. When unappreciated, one'd better cultivate his mind. When empowered, one'd better benefit mankind.

（王昌玲 译2）●●●

1. When poor, conduct yourself virtuously; when rich, contribute yourself generously.

（冯雷 译1）●●●

12. If you are poor and powerless, work to the betterment of yourself; if you are rich and powerful, work to the betterment of the world.

（冯雷 译2）★●

13. Resist temptation in poverty and assist the poor in wealth.

（艾朝阳 译）★

【59】尽信书则不如无书。——《孟子·尽心下》

投票：外方评委8人投票★，中方评委4人投票●

1. Be a critical reader.

（王成杰 译）★★★★★●●

2. It is ridiculous to trust every word in the book.

（董庆瑗 译）★★●

3. Do cast a critical eye on whatever books you read.

（王毅 译）★●●

4. A blind belief in books is worse than reading no books at all.

（王昌玲 译）●●●

5. Don't take anything blindly.

（陶家乐 译）★●

6. Books do more harm than good if they are swallowed, but not digested.

（吴春晓 译）★★

7. Better to read no books than to believe in every word in the books.

（艾朝阳 译）●●

8. I'd rather have no book than blindly accept everything contained in books.

（叶如钢 译）★

9. Believing everything one reads is more dangerous than not reading anything at all.

（石爱伟 译）★

10. Reading uncritically is even worse than not reading at all.

（田璐 译）★

11. When reading, things should be viewed in a dialectical way for even classics have fallacies.

（王婷 译）★

【60】不以规矩，不能成方圆。——《孟子·离娄上》

投票：外方评委6人投票★，中方评委5人投票●

1. No common rules, no fair games.

（杨中仁 译） ★●●●

2. Rules get things done.

（王成杰 译） ★●

3. No rules, no order.

（王毅 译） ★●

4. Rules and norms make things right.

（丁如伟 译） ★★

5. Respect the standards.

（陶家乐 译） ★★

6. Disciplines help one make achievements.

（曹小菁 译） ●●

7. Nothing can be done without rules or standards.

（马建军 译） ●●

8. Without rules, nothing can be done well.

（王昌玲 译） ●●

9. With the ruler, men draw straight lines; by the rules, men do right things.

（吴春晓 译） ●●

10. One cannot draw a perfect circle without a compass.

（杨胜悦 译） ★

11. It's the discipline that leads to success.

（张晓阳 译） ★

【61】人有不为也，而后可以有为。——《孟子·离娄下》

投票：外方评委7人投票★，中方评委4人投票●

1. To make accomplishments, one has to make sacrifices.

(何艳 译) ★ ★ ★ ★ ★ ●

2. Only by getting rid of trivial things can we concentrate on fulfilling the great target.

(郁序新 译) ★ ★ ★ ● ●

3. Abandon what is beyond your power and focus on what is within your power to make a great feat.

(倪庆行 译) ★ ●

4. Great accomplishments start from giving up on trivialities.

(樊功生 译) ★ ●

5. You have to give up certain things in order to do what you should do.

(王如利 译) ★ ●

6. Some things need to be sacrificed so other things can flourish.

(陶家乐 译) ★

7. One should choose what not to do in order to do well.

(冯雷 译) ★

8. Some things must be left undone.

(杨胜悦 译) ★

【62】天将降大任于斯人也，必先苦其心志，劳其筋骨，饿其体肤，空乏其身，行拂乱其所为，所以动心忍性，曾益其所不能。

——《孟子·告子下》

投票：外方评委11人投票★，中方评委2人投票●

1. There is no success without hardship. God delivers man a sense of mission and teaches them how to challenge the spiritual pain, physical suffering and all kinds of adversity in life.

(郁序新 译) ★ ★ ★ ★ ★

2. God will test you with harsh conditions to build you up.

(陶家乐 译) ★ ★ ★

3. When Heaven invests a person with great responsibilities, it first builds his resilience and maximizes his full potential through a variety of physical and mental adversities.

(何冰 译) ★ ★ ★

4. When Heaven is about to bestow a grand mission on a man, it will first torture his heart and soul, labor his sinews and bones, starve his body and flesh, impoverish him and impede his deeds, so as to spur his heart, steel his nature, and strengthen his abilities.

(王如利 译) ★ ●

5. When a man is destined to be a great leader, he'll be tested on the following attributes: fortitude, forbearance, strength and attentiveness. He will have to face adversaries, stand toil, fatigue and hunger, and fight off distractions from his cause. From these tests, he emerges as more dauntless, patient, focused and competent.

(吴春晓 译) ★ ★

6. Behold the omens of grand missions: upsetting adversity, back-breaking toil; starvation, deprivation and frustration untold, all to stimulate, temper and strengthen the staunch soul.

（张建惠 译）★★

7. When God intends to entrust a person with a great task, he will first bring him pain, toil, hunger, poverty and bad luck so as to make him strong and enhance his abilities.

（王成杰 译）★

8. When heaven is to entrust a man with great responsibilities, it will frustrate him, exhaust him, starve him, hinder his efforts, and leave him impoverished. Only in this way can his mind be enlightened, his tolerance developed and his weaknesses turned into strengths.

（冯雷 译）★

9. Before giving them great tasks, Heaven sends all kind of sufferings to those it chooses. By doing so, it well toughens them from body to soul, and from ability to willpower.

（铁冰 译）★

【63】夏虫不可以语于冰者，笃于时也。

——《庄子·外篇·秋水》

投票：外方评委5人投票★，中方评委5人投票●

1. Don't waste your breath talking about ice with summer insects who have never experienced cold.

（王昌玲 译1）★●●●●

2. Never waste time talking about winter ice with summer insects, because their horizons are limited by the season.

（张俊锋 译）●●●●●

3. Don't talk about winter ice with a summer insect who never lives to see it.

（石永浩 译）★●●●

4. We can't talk about ice with insects of summer because they can't live till winter(or they're limited by the weather).

（魏红霞 译）●●●●

5. A person's knowledge is subject to his life experience.

（杨秀波 译）★★★

6. Never discuss ice with summer insects who never live to winter.

（彭智鹏 译）●●●

7. Summer insects cannot be convinced of the existence of ice.

（王昌玲 译2）★★

8. It is fruitless to make a summer worm to understand what ice is like, for its short life cycle has never extended to winter at all.

（石爱伟 译）●●

9. The knowledge as well as a talk is time-confined.

（艾朝阳 译）★

10. We cannot talk about ice with summer insects, that relates to the cold season.

（赵宜忠 译）★

11. Don't ever initiate a conversation between summer insects and ice: they are not of the same season, nor are they on the same page.

（王绍昌 译）★

【64】哀莫大于心死。——《庄子·外篇·田子方》

投票：外方评委7人投票★，中方评委7人投票●

1. No sorrow is deeper than utter despair.

（张晓阳 译）★★★●●●●●

2. Nothing saddens people more than a withered heart.

（王绍昌 译1）★●●●●●●

3. Despair is the greatest sorrow.

（王绍昌 译2）★★★★●●

4. No woe is more wretched than a dead heart.

（刘群 译）★★★●●

5. Nothing is sadder in the world than the loss of hope and expectation for anything.

（杨秀波 译）★★●●

6. No sorrow is greater than the heart being numbed by despair.

（石永浩 译）●●●●

7. No sorrow is greater than abandoning all interests in the world.

（石爱伟 译1）★●

8. Nothing is more lamentable than a dead heart.

（郁序新 译）★●

9. Nothing can be sadder than being down in the dumps.

（魏红霞 译）●●

10. With the heart's demise, the greatest grief will arise.

（倪庆行 译）●●

11. Alas, my heart's dead! No more grief than this.

（彭智鹏 译）●●

12. Indifference is the worst attitude toward life.

（石爱伟 译2）★

【65】路漫漫其修远兮，吾将上下而求索。——屈原《离骚》

投票：外方评委 13 人投票★，中方评委 15 人投票●

1. The road to truth is long and rough, but my perseverance to seek is strong and tough.

（王国己 译）★★★★★★●●●●●●●●●●

2. The path ahead is long and narrow, yet I will pursue truth high and low to its very marrow!

（倪庆行 译）★★★★●●●●●●●●●●

3. The road ahead is long and hard to navigate, but I will take it with passion and determination to achieve my dream.

（冯雷 译）★★★★★★★●●●

4. The way is endless, but my will is relentless.

（艾朝阳 译1）★★★●●●●●●●

5. The way ahead is so long without ending, yet high and low I'll search with my will unbending.

（任诚刚 译）★●●●●●

6. The way is long and long; my effort goes on and on.

（曹小菁 译）★★★●●

7. The way to truth is very long, I will seek on and on.

（孟朝岗 译）★●●●●

8. No matter how far and tortuous the road ahead, I shall explore seeking my ideal till I'm dead.

（王昌玲 译）★★●●

9. The way is far and the chance is slim, but I'll go up and down to reach for the truth.

（艾朝阳 译2）★●●●

10. My way ahead is long and winding, yet high and low, I will seek with my will unbending.

（许霖越 译）●●●●

11. There far beyond, oh, lies my goal, I'll seek it with body and soul.

（程永生 译）●●●

12. The destination is nowhere near; I shall forge on for the ideal dear.

（石永浩 译）●●

13. Oh, the road is long, and deep I'll seek along.

（彭智鹏 译）●●

14. The way ahead is rough and tough; I will persist in toil and moil.

（王绍昌 译）●●

【66】青，取之于蓝，而青于蓝；冰，水为之，而寒于水。

——《荀子·劝学》

投票：外方评委5人投票★，中方评委5人投票●

1. As indigo is bluer than the indigo plant and ice is colder than water, the student can surpass the teacher.

（乐国斌 译）★★●●●

2. Just as indigo is taken from indigo plants but bluer and ice is derived from water but colder, so a fine pupil shall outshine his master.

（张俊锋 译）★★★●

3. Darker than blue, but out of blue, green develops; colder than water, but out of water, ice develops.

（程永生 译）★●●

4. Indigo is extracted from yet bluer than indigo plant, and ice, coming from water, colder; the pupil is to the master what indigo is to the plant, ice to water.

（张琼 译）★ ★

5. Just as indigo extracted from the plant is bluer than the plant, so is ice colder than water.

（许霖越 译）● ●

6. Indigo is extracted from bluegrass, but bluer than bluegrass. Ice is water frozen but colder than water.

（王昌玲 译）● ●

7. Indigo is bluer, ice is colder; the young outrun the elder, students overtake their master.

（冯雷 译）● ●

8. Indigo extracted from blue is darker than blue; ice frozen by water is colder than water.

（倪庆行 译）★

9. Ice coming from water is colder than water. One learning from his teacher can be more learned than the latter.

（铁冰 译）★

10. Extracted from blue, cyan is finer than blue; formed from water, ice is colder than water.

（叶如钢 译）★

【67】道虽迩，不行不至；事虽小，不为不成。

——《荀子·修身》

投票：外方评委10人投票★，中方评委4人投票●

1. Even the smallest goals require action.

（陶家乐 译） ★ ★ ★ ★ ★ ● ● ●

2. Without walking, even a short distance can't be covered; without action, even an easy task cannot be done.

（杨秀波 译） ★ ★ ★ ● ●

3. Action is the key even to a small task, whether a short journey or a simple errand.

（刘向军 译） ★ ★ ★

4. Short as the journey is, the destination cannot be reached without taking steps. Trivial as the matter is, the task cannot be accomplished without taking actions.

（倪庆行 译） ★ ★ ●

5. Even if the distance is short, you cannot reach the end without a walk; even if the thing is small, you cannot complete it with just a talk.

（任诚刚 译） ● ●

6. The least distance still wears toes; the easiest task calls for efforts.

（吴春晓 译） ● ●

7. However close truth is, we can't attain it without efforts; however simple a task is, we can't finish it without action.

（王毅 译） ● ●

8. There is no way to success without a try, like none of pie falling from the sky.

（郁序新 译） ● ●

9. You will reach nowhere without taking a first step though the destination is near; you will achieve nothing without taking action though the task is fiddling.

（刘群 译） ●●

10. The shortest distance can't be covered if one does not walk; the slightest thing can't be achieved if one fails to act.

（何艳 译） ★

11. Walking gets you anywhere, far or near; working gets everything done, big or small.

（叶步青 译） ★

【68】谣言止于智者。

——语本《荀子·大略》："流言止于知者。"

投票：外方评委7人投票★，中方评委2人投票●

1. Rumors are not passed on by the wise.

（叶如钢 译） ★ ★ ★

2. The wise don't spread rumors.

（魏红霞 译） ★ ★ ★

3. The wise won't circulate rumors.

（董庆瑗 译） ★ ★ ●

4. Rumor stops before the wise.

（王昌玲 译） ★ ●

5. Rumors stop with the wise.

（马建军、王绍昌 译） ★ ●

6. Wisdom is the bane of rumors.

（丁如伟 译）★ ●

7. A rumor dies when it reaches the ears of a wise man.

（刘雪芹 译）★ ●

8. The wise buy no rumors.

（杨胜悦 译）★ ●

9. The wise and virtuous man is no transmitter of rumors.

（石爱伟 译）★

10. Gossip dies when it hits a wise person's ears.

（王梅兰 译，引用）★

11. A wise man stops a rumor.

（任诚刚 译）★

12. Intelligent people know to not pass on rumors.

（陶家乐 译）★

13. The wise turn a deaf ear to rumours.

（何冰 译）★

14. In the ears of the wise, a rumor dies.

（石永浩 译）★

15. The wise never spread the rumors.

（吴冰 译）★

16. A wise man will stop spreading a rumor.

（董秀静 译）★

17. Rumors are terminated by the sage.

（何艳 译）★

【69】 万物各得其和以生，各得其养以成。——《荀子·天论》

投票：外方评委9人投票★，中方评委5人投票●

1. Everything in nature grows and thrives in accordance with the law of heaven and earth.

（石爱伟 译）★★★★★★★●

2. All living things need the right environment and nourishment for their birth and growth.

（王成杰 译）★★★★●

3. All beings flourish when they live in harmony and receive nourishment from nature.

（任诚刚 译,引用）★★●

4. Harmonious coexistence and mutual benefit make everything grow and flourish.

（丁如伟 译）★●●

5. In concord with nature, things are born and nurtured.

（吴春晓 译）★★★

6. All beings should be in harmony with nature in order to survive, and obtain from nature the nurture in order to thrive.

（马建军 译）●●

7. All things live and grow in harmony; all things are nourished and thus thrive.

（何艳 译）●●

8. For all things on earth, when conditions permit they come into being; with nourishment they grow and thrive.

（田璐 译）★

【70】锲而舍之，朽木不折；锲而不舍，金石可镂。

——《荀子·劝学》

投票：外方评委 7 人投票★，中方评委 5 人投票●

1. Perseverance is the key to success.

（王昌玲 译）★★★●●

2. If you carve but give up half way, even a decayed piece of wood will not break; if you carve persistently, even metal and stone can be engraved.

（曹小菁 译）★★●●●

3. Without perseverance, all efforts will be wasted; with perseverance, nothing is unattainable.

（王如利 译）★★★

4. With perseverance, you can carve metal and stone. Otherwise, you can't even break a rotten log.

（王成杰 译）★●●

5. If you stop carving halfway, you can't even break the rotten wood; but if you keep carving, you can even engrave metal and stone.

（张晓阳 译）●●●

6. If one quits easily, even the rotten wood can't be broken. If one perseveres, even the metal and stone can be carved.

（何艳 译）●●●

7. What is important is to be persistent to the end. Without this spirit, nothing can be done.

（郁序新 译）★★

8. Perseverance leads to success.

（王慧玉 译）★●

名言警句英译

9. Carve but quit halfway, even a decayed piece of wood refuses to break; carve with persistence, even metal and stone can be engraved.

（倪庆行 译）★

10. With perseverance, metal and stone can be whittled; without perseverance, even decayed wood defies whittling.

（乐国斌 译）★

11. With perseverance, you can craft a piece of gold. Without, you can't even break a rotten log.

（王梅兰 译）★

12. A rotten wood would be unbreakable if one gives up easily, the hardest rock could be readily carved if one persists.

（樊功生 译）★

13. With perseverance, even hard metal or stones could be carved, but without it, even decayed wood could not be broken, which means nothing could be achieved.

（杨秀波 译）★

【71】其曲弥高，其和弥寡。——宋玉《对楚王问》

投票：外方评委 11 人投票★，中方评委 8 人投票●

1. The more difficult the tune, the fewer the players.

（魏红霞 译）★★★★★★★★

2. The more profound a tune sounds, the fewer followers it finds.

（倪庆行 译）★★●●●●

3. The higher tune, the fewer followers.

（彭智鹏 译）●●●●

4. The more abstruse the idea, the fewer the followers.

（王昌玲 译）★●●

5. The more refined a style of music, the fewer followers.

（冯雷 译1）★★★

6. High tunes find few singers.

（石爱伟 译）●●●

7. Highbrow melodies have fewer echoes or followers.

（王绍昌 译）●●●

8. High sophistication is not a crowd pleaser.

（樊功生 译）★●

9. The more elegant and recondite a tune is, fewer followers it attracts.

（段冰知 译1）★●

10. The more sophisticated an artistic conception, the fewer admirers.

（冯雷 译2）★★

11. The more highbrow you are, the fewer appreciators you have.

（铁冰 译）●●

12. Too highbrow a tune gets too few singers in chorus.

（张俊锋 译）●●

13. The higher the pitch is, the harder the chorus will be. (It's hard for ordinary people to understand what elites think.)

（张晔 译）●●

14. The extraordinary melody finds a rare chord.

（艾朝阳 译）★

15. An elegant tune has appreciators few.

（段冰知 译2）★

【72】事以密成，语以泄败。——韩非《韩非子·说难》

投票：外方评委6人投票★，中方评委5人投票●

1. Silence propels achievements. Gossips give birth to failures.

（王梅兰 译） ★★●●

2. Secrecy holds the key to many successful undertakings.

（马百亮 译） ★●●●

3. A loose tongue may cause failure of a mission.

（冯雷 译） ★●●●

4. Secrecy secures success.

（田璐 译） ★●●

5. Things in secret will be safely accomplished, and a slip of the tongue may cause failure.

（杨中仁 译） ★●

6. Secret plans are the best plans to success.

（何冰 译） ★★

7. Holding your tongue may bring you success, but breathing a word may bring you failure.

（张晓阳 译） ●●

8. Plots succeed only when kept secret, while unguarded words lead to failure.

（叶如钢 译） ●●

9. What's in secret succeeds; what's revealed fails.

（乐国斌 译） ★

10. You won't succeed if you boast.

（瑞雪 译） ★

【73】不知而自以为知，百祸之宗也。

——吕不韦《吕氏春秋·览·有始览》

投票：外方评委8人投票★，中方评委5人投票●

1. Not knowing your own ignorance is the root of all misfortune.

（王成杰 译）★★★★★●

2. To be ignorant of one's ignorance is the bane of all banes.

（吴春晓 译）★★★●●

3. Ignorance is the root of misfortunes, and even more so when it's unrecognized.

（叶如钢 译）★★★●

4. The ignorance of ignorance is the root of all disasters.

（王如利 译）★★●●●

5. The ignorance of ignorance is the source of disasters.

（马建军 译）★●●

6. Pretending to know what you actually do not know is the root of all disasters.

（倪庆行 译）★●

7. All woes stem from self-opinionated ignorance.

（乐国斌 译）★●

8. Ignorance of one's own limitations is the root of all human problems.

（冯雷 译）★★

9. Calamities will fall one after another upon him who is ignorant but pretends he is not.

（石爱伟 译）★

10. It is the very source of your sufferings that you think you know everything when you actually know nothing.

（王毅 译）★

名言警句英译

11. To think that you know something you actually don't know is the root of all disaster.

（董秀静 译）★

12. Feigned knowledge is the origin of various disasters.

（杨秀波 译）★

13. Not knowing that you don't know, this is the root of many troubles.

（何艳 译）★

【74】泰山不让土壤，故能成其大；河海不择细流，故能就其深。

——李斯《谏逐客书》

投票：外方评委 10 人投票★，中方评委 7 人投票●

1. Accepting each grain of sand makes the mountain high. Embracing every drop of water makes the ocean wide.

（张晔 译）★★★★★★★●●●●●●

2. Mount Tai is tall because it accommodates all types of soil and rock; the ocean is vast because it collects all waters around the clock.

（冯雷 译）★★★★★★★●●●

3. Refusing no earth, Mount Tai is high; deserting no trickle, the sea is wide.

（魏红霞 译）●●●●●

4. Mount Tai is so tall, because it never abandons any soil; rivers and seas are so deep and wide, because they never repel any stream and flow.

（郁序新 译）●●●●

5. Lofty mountains are lofty because they consist of multitudinous rocks and earth; vast oceans are vast because they comprise countless streams and rivers.

（石爱伟 译）★●●

6. Indiscriminate gathering creates great mountains and deep oceans.

（李开林 译）★ ★ ★

7. Mount Tai is grand because it rejects no soil nor gravel; the rivers and sea are deep since they take in all small streams.

（叶如钢 译）●●●

8. Mount Tai gives up no soil at all, so it can be so majestic and tall; the sea and rivers can be so deep and wide because they repel no rill small.

（赵宜忠 译）●●●

9. By stacking and stocking soils and land, Mount Tai becomes mighty, towering and sturdy; by mixing and mingling streams and brooks, rivers and seas turn deep, wide, and steady.

（王绍昌 译）★●

10. Mount Tai stands high, which is attributable to its conservation of countless soil; rivers lie deep, which is accreditable to their welcome of millions of trickles.

（艾朝阳 译）●●

11. Mount Tai rejects no soil, thus its height; the ocean welcomes all brooklets, thus its depth.

（王昌玲 译）★

第二篇
秦汉魏晋南北朝时期

Chapter II
Qin, Han, Wei, Jin, and Southern and Northern Dynasties

【75】树欲静而风不止，子欲养而亲不待。

——韩婴《韩诗外传》

投票：外方评委10人投票★，中方评委9人投票●

1. Trees wish to stay still, but winds blow against their will. Children wish to care, but parents are no longer there.

(刘亚木 译1) ★★●●●●●●●

2. Trees desire to stand still, but the wind keeps trees sway; children expect to show their filial piety, but parents long turned to clay.

(王绍昌 译) ★★●●●●●

3. Still trees want to stay, yet winds make them sway. Sons want to behave in a filial way, yet their parents have passed away.

(倪庆行 译) ★●●●●●●

4. Winds are blowing, trees have nowhere to hide; parents are aging, sons should be on their side. Yet trees always fret, and sons always regret.

(冯雷 译) ★★★●

5. The trees want to stay still but the winds disagree; the children want to show filial piety but their parents disappear.

(艾朝阳 译) ★★●

6. Trees want to stay still, while the wind keep blowing. Children want to be filial, yet time is not waiting.

(徐艺玮 译) ●●●

7. Winds allow not trees to stand still. Time allows not aged parents to wait for their children's requiting.

(铁冰 译) ★●

8. Trees want quietness, but winds last; children want to care, but their parents have passed.

（刘亚木 译2）★●

【76】**喜名者必多怨，好誉者必多侮**。——韩婴《韩诗外传》

投票：外方评委8人投票★，中方评委4人投票●

1. Chasing fame invites hatred; seeking praise incurs insult.

（石永浩 译1）★★★★★★★★★●●●
2. Seeking fame often spells resentment. Pursuing glory usually causes humiliation.

（张晔 译）★★★★★●●
3. He who is addicted to fame is often resentful; he who is obsessed with honor often swallows an insult.

（石爱伟 译）★★●●
4. Fame pursuers usually harbor complaints, and praise seekers often receive insults.

（叶如钢 译1）●●●
5. Many hate those who seek fame and put vain men to shame.

（魏红霞 译）●●
6. Fame may trigger jealousy; infamy may await vanity.

（石永浩 译2）●●
7. Lovers of fame must be blamed, likers of praise must be shamed.

（杨中仁 译）●●

8. Thirst for fame causes resentment; hunger for name swallows humiliation.

（冯雷 译）●●

9. Those who indulge in fame are much resented, those who seek praises are often insulted.

（叶如钢 译2）★

【77】爱出者爱返，福往者福来。——贾谊《新书》

投票：外方评委7人投票★，中方评委3人投票●

1. Those who give love gather love. Those who offer blessings receive blessings.

（王如利 译）★★★●

2. Love and blessings always find their way back.

（冯雷 译）★★●●

3. Those who love will be loved in return; those who bless will be blessed in return.

（乐国斌 译）★★★★

4. Love tendered, love received; blessings sown, blessings reaped.

（倪庆行 译）★★●

5. Whoever offers others love will be rewarded with love; whoever makes others happy will be rewarded with happiness.

（张晓阳 译）★●

6. Those who offer love and kindness will receive them as rewards in return.

（王毅 译）★●

7. Love and you'll be loved in return. Share your blessings and they'll multiply.

（马建军 译）★

8. The one offering love will be loved. One giving happiness will reap happiness.

（杨秀波 译）★

【78】塞翁失马，焉知非福。——刘安《淮南子·人间训》

投票：外方评委11人投票★，中方评委5人投票●

1. Some loss may turn out to be a blessing in disguise.

（石爱伟 译）★★★★★●●●●

2. Losses now can turn out to be blessings later.

（王绍昌 译）★★★★★★★★

3. The old man lost his horse, a bad day? Perhaps not! Good fortune came his way.

（冯雷 译1）★●●●

4. The loss of a horse may prove to be a blessing in disguise.

（张顺生 译）●●

5. A loss can be a blessing in disguise. A gain may end up in a bad surprise.

（王昌玲 译）●●

6. Misfortune or good fortune knows only God, yet loss unexpectedly turns jackpot.

（郁序新 译）●●

7. Horse lost, fortune procured.

（曹小菁 译）● ●

8. Fortune and misfortune are turning the wheel of life, so come what may!

（冯雷 译2）● ●

9. When the old man lost his horse, who knows it's not a blessing?

（任诚刚 译）★

10. A loss might get you away from a disaster that would have happened.

（李开林 译）★

11. An old man near the border lost his horse. Isn't it a blessing in disguise?

（杨秀波 译）★

12. Loss can lead to gain.

（叶如钢 译）★

【79】梧桐一叶落，天下尽知秋。

——语本刘安《淮南子·说山训》："一叶落而知岁之将暮。"

投票：外方评委8人投票★，中方评委5人投票●

1. Once the leaves begin to fall, we know autumn's here with us all.

（冯雷 译）★ ★ ★ ★ ★ ★ ★ ●

2. When parasol leaves fall, the coming of autumn is known to all.

（石永浩 译）★ ● ● ●

3. When a leaf from the wutong tree falls, autumn has arrived.

（瑞雪 译）★ ★ ●

4. A single falling leaf heralds the arrival of autumn.

（樊功生 译）★●●

5. Seeing a parasol leave swirling down, one can tell autumn is coming to town.

（吴春晓 译）●●●

6. Once the leaves of phoenix trees begin to fall, the harbinger of autumn will be noticed by all.

（张晓阳 译）★●

7. A single leaf falling from the parasol tree tells the arrival of autumn.

（王绍昌 译）★●

8. Just as a falling leaf indicates that autumn is coming, something big can be deduced from small things through keen observation and feeling.

（董秀静 译）★★

9. A falling leaf from a tree forecasts to all that it's the beginning of the season fall.

（石爱伟 译）★

10. When a phoenix tree leaf falls, all in the land know it's autumn.

（叶如钢 译）★

【80】智者千虑必有一失，愚者千虑必有一得。

——司马迁《史记·淮阴侯列传》

投票：外方评委8人投票★，中方评委12人投票●

1. The wise are not always wise; the foolish are not always foolish.

（石永浩 译1）★★★●●●●●●●

2. Even the wisest sometimes errs; even the dumbest sometimes scores.

(乐国斌 译1) ●●●●●●●

3. No wise men never blunders; no fools always errs.

(石永浩 译2) ●●●●●●●

4. Once in a thousand times a wise man blunders and a fool's wits shine.

(叶如钢 译1) ★★★★★

5. A fox may fall into a trap; a donkey may escape a kill.

(冯雷 译) ●●●

6. A wise man may err; a fool may gain.

(任诚刚 译) ●●●

7. Once in a while, the wise blunder and the dumb get it right.

(叶如钢 译2) ★●

8. There is always something that even the smartest brain can't cover while a lesser might consider.

(李开林 译) ★●

9. There is no Solomon but will err; there is no fool but can think up a good idea.

(张俊锋 译) ●●

10. Thousands of considerations may witness a wise man lose once and a fool gain once.

(程永生 译) ●●

11. Nobody is wise at all times; nobody is foolish at all times.

(乐国斌 译2) ★

【81】 狭路相逢勇者胜，势均力敌谋者成。

——语本司马迁《史记·廉颇蔺相如列传》："其道远险狭，譬之犹两鼠斗于穴中，将勇者胜。"

投票：外方评委8人投票★，中方评委7人投票●

1. In a narrow path encounter, whoever is braver wins; in a nip and tuck battle, whoever is wiser prevails.

（张晓阳 译）★●●●●

2. Confronted on a narrow path, the brave wins; strength well-matched, a strategist succeeds.

（魏红霞 译）●●●●●

3. The fearless conquer in a close combat, the savvy prevail between matching rivals.

（樊功生 译）●●●●●

4. A brave man wins in a tight fight, but a mastermind wins in a nip and tuck combat.

（杨中仁 译）●●●●

5. On the narrow battlefield, a brave man will win; in a close contest, a good strategist will triumph.

（彭智鹏 译）★★●

6. In an unavoidable confrontation fortune favours the bold; in a well-matched situation fortune favours the wise.

（冯雷 译）★●●

7. Bravery solves a confrontation on a narrow bridge while scheme ends a close game.

（李开林 译）★●●

8. Being cornered on the ring, one may save the day with valor; being rivalled in strength, one may turn the tide with tactics.

（石永浩 译）★ ★ ★

9. Bravery or strategy makes a person outshine his or her equal.

（杨秀波 译）★ ★ ★

10. In a skirmish valor prevails; in a stalemate stratagem wins.

（石爱伟 译1）● ● ●

11. In a close battle, the smarter wins. In a fancy battle, the fiercer wins.

（艾朝阳 译）★ ★

12. Confronted in peril, the braver one wins; equally matched, the schemer conquers.

（王昌玲 译）● ●

13. Strength being equal, it is valor and stratagem that decides the outcome of the battle.

（石爱伟 译2）★

【82】当断不断，反受其乱。——司马迁《史记·春申君列传》

投票：外方评委7人投票★，中方评委6人投票●

1. Sometimes hesitation causes regretful consequences.

（石爱伟 译）★ ★ ★ ★ ★ ★ ★

2. Hesitation heralds disasters.

（石永浩 译）★ ★ ★ ★ ● ●

3. Disasters will arise if one hesitates when it's time for him to decide.

（魏红霞 译1）★ ● ● ● ●

4. Be decisive in time or you shall suffer in no time.

（王昌玲 译1） ●●●●

5. Indecision at a decisive moment induces disaster.

（铁冰 译） ★★●

6. Timely decision shall save one endless trouble.

（王昌玲 译2） ★●●

7. It is the seed of later disaster to leave behind what should be eradicated.

（杨秀波 译） ●●●

8. Indecision entails a great risk.

（樊功生 译） ★●

9. At a critical moment, irresolution will lead to irreversible consequences.

（冯雷 译1） ★●

10. Hesitance at a crucial moment always ends up misfortune.

（郁序新 译） ●●

11. Act promptly, or it'll be deadly.

（魏红霞 译2） ●●

12. Catch the decisive moment, end it or be troubled more after.

（李开林 译） ●●

13. Indecisiveness kills at a decisive moment.

（冯雷 译2） ★

14. A stitch in time saves nine, with the rear secure.

（赵宜忠 译） ★

15. A delayed decision harms.

（曹小菁 译） ★

【83】得人者兴，失人者崩。——司马迁《史记·商君列传》

投票：外方评委6人投票★，中方评委6人投票●

1. He who wins support will flourish; he who loses support will perish.

（崔传明 译）★★●●●

2. Popularity is the key to prosperity.

（田璐 译）★★●

3. With people, you prosper; without, you falter.

（孙壮 译）★★★

4. If a state wins the hearts of its people, it will thrive. If not, it will perish.

（王成杰 译）★●

5. Supported by people, a nation rises and prospers, while deserted by people, it falls apart.

（艾朝阳 译）★●

6. With people supporting you, you will thrive; without people supporting you, you won't survive.

（倪庆行 译）●●

7. People's support decides the rise and fall of a government.

（王毅 译）●●

8. Support from people makes one prosperous; losing support leads one to failure.

（陶家乐 译）●●

9. A nation which wins support from people thrives; a nation which loses support from people crumbles.

（丁如伟 译）●●

10. Those who win the support of people prosper, and those who lose perish.

（王婷 译）●●

11. People's support is vital to the rise and fall of any nation or any political power.

（史红霞 译）★

12. People's support is the first priority of a nation's prosperity.

（魏红霞 译）★

【84】 天下熙熙，皆为利来；天下攘攘，皆为利往。

——司马迁《史记·货殖列传》

投票：外方评委9人投票★，中方评委5人投票●

1. All the hustle and bustle of this world is driven by the desire for gain.

（马百亮 译）★★★★★★●

2. Behind all the hustle and bustle in life, money rattles.

（吴春晓 译）★★●●

3. Why all the hustle and bustle? Profit, nothing but profit.

（王昌玲 译）★●●

4. The hustle and bustle of the world is no more than exchanges of interests.

（田璐 译）★★★

5. Be it hustle or bustle in the world, all hinges upon benefits.

（倪庆行 译）●●●

6. In this bustling world, people come and go, pursuing their own interests.

（马建军 译）★●

7. Hustling and bustling, all are for the pursuit of interests.

（张晓阳 译）★●

8. The world does things for profit.

（瑞雪 译）★★

9. This world is but a vanity fair.

（王成杰 译）●●

10. For fame and fortune, people come bustling and go rustling.

（崔传明 译）●●

11. For benefit, people come and go; for profit, human crowds flow.

（冯雷 译）●●

12. The whole world is bustling and hustling for profit.

（乐国斌 译）★

13. People all over the world flock in and rush out for profit.

（任诚刚 译）★

【85】乘人之车者载人之患，衣人之衣者怀人之忧，食人之食者死人之事。

——司马迁《史记·淮阴侯列传》

投票：外方评委7人投票★，中方评委3人投票●

1. When you ride in his carriage, share his sorrows; when you wear his clothes, share his worries; when you eat his food, serve him with all your might.

（王成杰 译）★★★●●●

2. Riding in someone's wagon, one should help to overcome his adversity. Wearing someone's clothes, one should care about his worries. Having meals provided by someone, one should be ready to fight to the death for him.

（叶如钢 译）★★★●●

3. If a person provides you with a vehicle, clothing, and food, you are supposed to share his troubles and worries, and even pledge your life to defend him.

（何艳 译）★●●

4. If you want to enjoy others' fruits, you've got to share their labor.

（王昌玲 译）★★★

5. To those people who help you meet the basic needs like food or clothing, return the favor with all you might.

（何冰 译）★★★

6. Wherever you are, you must learn to be grateful to the benefactor with your action.

（郁序新 译）★

7. Share worries, bear hardships and face challenges with those who provide you with food, clothes and transport.

（冯雷 译）★

8. Charioted by others, you should share their disasters; clad by others, you should concern their worries; fed by others, you should go all out to work for them.

（倪庆行 译）●

9. To ride in a man's car is to share his troubles. To wear his clothes is to share his sorrows. And to eat his food is to share his missions.

（马建军 译）●

10. When enjoying the benefits provided, one should repay the providers by addressing their concerns.

（王毅 译）●

【86】食必常饱，然后求美；衣必常暖，然后求丽；居必常安，然后求乐。

——刘向《说苑·反质》

投票：外方评委 10 人投票★，中方评委 7 人投票●

1. Well-fed, one seeks taste in food; well-clad, one pursues design in dress; well-sheltered, one chases comfort in housing.

（王绍昌 译1）● ● ● ● ● ● ●

2. One would seek a finer taste when abundant in food, fancy a better style when adequate in clothing, and pursue enjoyment when comfortable in accommodation.

（樊功生 译）● ● ● ● ● ●

3. Belly-filled, people start to think of delicacies; body-covered, people begin to yearn for elegance; roof-secured, people begin to look for fancies.

（王绍昌 译2）● ● ● ● ● ●

4. In matters of food, clothing and shelter, the basic need must be satisfied before any talk of fashion or luxury.

（石爱伟 译1）★ ★ ★ ★ ★ ●

5. He who doesn't have enough to eat doesn't seek taste in food; he who doesn't have enough to wear doesn't seek beauty in clothing; he who doesn't have a roof over his head doesn't seek comfort in shelter.

（石爱伟 译2）★ ● ● ● ●

6. Eating his fill, one pursues delicacy; warmly dressed, he pursues finery; living safely, he pursues gaiety.

（魏红霞 译）★ ★ ★ ●

7. One must always be decently-fed before seeking delicacy; one must always be warmly dressed before seeking splendor; one must always be living in peace before seeking bliss.

（倪庆行 译）★●●

8. In our daily pursuit, more often quantity first, and quality second. If we have no worry about food supply, we can ask for better tastes. If we have no worry about clothing, we can be critical about its fashion. If we have no worry about dwelling place, we can arrange more facilities for entertainments.

（艾朝阳 译）★ ★ ★

9. If having been well fed, clothed and sheltered, people naturally expect life to be more beautiful.

（石永浩 译）★ ★ ★

10. Delicacy comes after your hunger is staved, finery after you are properly dressed, and joyful life after you are comfortably sheltered.

（刘群 译）★●●

11. People start seeking delicacy after having enough food, fashion after enough clothing and entertainment after a decent residence.

（李开林 译）★

【87】士为知己者死，女为悦己者容。
——刘向《战国策·赵策一·晋毕阳之孙豫让》

投票：外方评委 9 人投票★，中方评委 10 人投票●

1. A warrior dies for his bosom friend; a lady dresses for her true admirer.

（王绍昌 译1）★ ★ ★ ★ ★ ★ ★ ●●

2. A man of honor could die for a bosom friend's cause; a woman beautifies herself for her lover's sake.

（石爱伟 译）●●●●●●

3. A gentleman will give his life to the one who knows him best; a lady will show her beauty to the one who wins her heart.

（丁立群 译）★★★★●●

4. A knight would die for his soul mate; a woman would doll herself up for her sweetheart.

（倪庆行 译）★●●●●●

5. A man of loyalty would die for a friend who shares his mind; a woman would primp for an admirer who wins her heart.

（冯雷 译）●●●●●

6. A true warrior would rather die for his devoting friend; a lady would try to become more graceful for the man who loves to bystand.

（郑晓春 译）★★●●

7. A gentleman would sacrifice his life for his bosom friends; a lady would enchant her wooers with her beauty.

（郁序新 译）★●●

8. Gentlemen would die for their appreciators; ladies would adorn for their admirers.

（王绍昌 译2）●●●

9. A man would die for a bosom friend, while a woman would dress up for her beloved.

（陈赛花 译）●●●

10. A real knight would not hesitate to die for the liege appreciating him; a fair lady may dress up for the one winning her heart.

（石永浩 译）●●

11. A man dies for one who deserves his loyalty; a woman primps for one who knows her beauty.

（王成杰 译）●●

12. A man would feel honored to die for the one who shares his weal and woe; a woman would feel pleased to prink for the one who adores her heart and soul.

（王毅 译）●●

13. A true man would die for his patron; a lady would smarten herself up for her admirer.

（刘群 译）★

【88】以财交者，财尽则交绝；以色交者，华落而爱渝。
——刘向《战国策·楚策一·江乙说于安陵君》

投票：外方评委 3 人投票★，中方评委 3 人投票●

1. Friendship based on money will perish when money runs out; love based on beauty will die when beauty withers away.

（马百亮 译）★★●●

2. Friendship based on wealth won't last; love out of lust dies fast.

（董庆瑗 译）★★●●

3. A relationship built upon money is fragile; a relationship only upon sexual appeal won't last long.

（石爱伟 译）★★●

4. Friendship based on money will come to an end when money runs out; love derived from lust for beauty will evaporate when beauty withers.

（倪庆行 译）★●

5. If fostered on wealth, friendship will be gone when wealth runs out; if built on beauty, love will be gone when beauty fades away.

(石永浩 译) ★ ●

6. Mercenary friends will take wings once your wealth runs up; beauty-lovers will betray you when your charm fades away.

(张俊锋 译) ★ ●

7. Friendship forged upon money will vanish the moment money is squandered. Likewise, love obtained upon beauty will vaporize the moment beauty fades.

(王昌玲 译) ● ●

8. Friendship can't be bought, nor can love be won with beauty. Bought friendship ends when money runs out and adulterated love abates as beauty fades.

(吴春晓 译) ★

9. Money makes friends, friends go gone once money goes gone. Appearance appeals to lover. Love switches once appearance withers.

(彭智鹏 译) ★

10. Relationships based on money terminate when money is exhausted; love based on sex shifts when beauty disappears.

(王绍昌 译) ★

11. Those who take advantage of money to make friends will lose their friends when their money runs out; those who get married for beauty will lose affection for their spouses when beauty withers away in old age.

(董秀静 译) ★

【89】父母之爱子，则为之计深远。

——刘向《战国策·赵策四·触龙说赵太后》

投票：外方评委 2 人投票★，中方评委 5 人投票●

1. Parents should help their children find the meaning of life and prepare for the future.

（冯雷 译）★★●

2. Loving parents plan far ahead for their children.

（叶如钢 译）★●●

3. If you love your kids, you would plan for their future with a vision.

（王梅兰 译）●●●

4. Parents who genuinely love their child will plan for their child's future.

（瑞雪 译）●●●

5. Parents who love their children should make long-term plans for them instead of focusing on immediate gains and losses.

（倪庆行 译）★●

6. The wise love from parents is to make long-term plans for their kids.

（王毅 译）★●

7. If you love your children, you should prepare them well for their future.

（马百亮 译）●●

8. Parental love means taking a long-range view for children.

（何艳 译）●●

9. Doting parents, if they really love their children, ought to prepare them for the future rather than meet all their present needs.

（石爱伟 译）★

【90】 聪者听于无声，明者见于未形。

——班固《汉书·伍被传》

投票：外方评委6人投票★，中方评委17人投票●

1. A wise man can hear the inaudible；a smart man can see the invisible.

（彭智鹏 译）★★★★★●●●●

2. A sharp listener can hear the wind before it comes，and a keen watcher can see the storm before it arrives.

（艾朝阳 译1）★★★●●●●●

3. Keen hearers can hear the inaudible；keen viewers can see the intangible.

（倪庆行 译）★★★●●●

4. Good ears hear in silence. Good eyes see in invisibility.

（孟朝岗 译）●●●●●●

5. Using his mind to hear and see，is a master's master key.

（冯雷 译1）★★★●

6. A man with perception hears the sound before it is made；a man with insight sees the shape before it is formed.

（冯雷 译2）★●●●

7. The sage hear without listening；the wise see without looking.

（石永浩 译1）●●●●

8. A good listener hears beyond words；a good viewer sees without signs.

（王如利 译）●●●●

9. The quick-eared hear what is unsaid；the sharp-eyed see what is unrevealed.

（李红雨 译）●●●●

10. A wise man can foresee everything and take actions.

（魏红霞 译）★★●

11. Those who can hear the thunder before it roars have sharp ears; those who can see the lightning before it flashes have keen eyes.

(艾朝阳 译2) ★ ★ ★

12. Good ears fore hear it where soundless; good eyes foresee it where form-less.

(石永浩 译2) ● ● ●

13. The wise perceive in silence, conceive in nihility.

(许霖越 译) ● ● ●

14. Foresight and insight make a Solomon.

(颜海峰 译1) ● ● ●

15. One who listens hears the silence; one who observes sees the invisible.

(王琳 译) ● ● ●

16. The wise see the inaudible and perceive the invisible.

(王绍昌 译) ● ● ●

17. The sapient can sense the soundless and sight the signless.

(颜海峰 译2) ● ●

18. The sagacious can hear sounds beforehand; the sapient can foresee things yet to happen.

(张俊锋 译) ● ●

19. He who hears the soundless and sees the formless is a real wise man.

(郭英杰 译) ● ●

【91】人固有一死，或重于泰山，或轻于鸿毛。

　　　　　　　　　　——班固《汉书·司马迁传》

投票：外方评委10人投票★，中方评委6人投票●

1. To die is human；to die for a noble cause outweighs a mountain，to die for nothing is light as a feather.

　　　　　　　　（张琼 译）★★★★●●●

2. We all die；but some people die for a noble purpose，while others die a death of triviality.

　　　　　　　　（石爱伟 译）★★★★★●

3. Life will end at its due time. Some dies dignified like a towering mountain，others expire meaninglessly like feathers in the wind.

　　　　　　　　（樊功生 译）★★★●●

4. Death is inevitable；some die adored and some die ignored.

　　　　　　　　（冯雷 译）●●●●●

5. Although one can't choose not to die，he can choose whether to die significantly or meaninglessly.

　　　　　　　　（曹小菁 译）★★●

6. No one is immortal，whose death is either greater than Mount Tai，or lighter than a feather.

　　　　　　　　（王勋 译）●●●

7. Death is beyond man，but to die worthy or unworthy he can plan.

　　　　　　　　（王昌玲 译1）★●

8. Death is inevitable. But one can die a worthless coward or a great hero.

　　　　　　　　（叶如钢 译）★●

9. Man will surely die，but some mean more than Mount Tai，while others mean less than feathers.

　　　　　　　　（魏红霞 译）★★

10. While death comes to all unavoidably, people die differently. Some die as splendidly as towering Mount Tai, while others expire as insignificantly as soft feathers in sky.

（王绍昌 译）★★

11. Human beings are subject to death, either worth millions of pounds or nothing at all.

（杨秀波 译）★

12. All men are equally mortal, yet some die heroic, others die small.

（王昌玲 译2）★

【92】以色事人者，色衰而爱弛，爱弛则恩绝。

——班固《汉书·孝武李夫人传》

投票：外方评委6人投票★，中方评委4人投票●

1. A woman who is favored because of her beauty will fall into disfavor when her beauty fades.

（王如利 译）★★★★★★●

2. The love and favor won by physical beauty will be lost with age.

（冯雷 译）★★★★★●

3. Affection and love gained for beautiful looks will fade away when the looks wither.

（叶如钢 译）★★★●●●

4. If a woman uses her beauty to win a man's love, the love diminishes and the affection ends as beauty fades away.

（马建军 译）★★★●●

5. Relationships based on looks will never last, for such a relationship breaks up when beautiful looks fade with age.

（吴春晓 译）★ ★ ●

6. Beauty is only skin deep and it can't be a preservative for love.

（王成杰 译）★ ★ ●

7. Your character and love shouldn't be based on beauty.

（陶家乐 译）★ ★ ★

8. Love relied on appearance cannot last forever.

（任诚刚 译）★ ★ ★

9. Love won with youthful beauty will fade away with it.

（石永浩 译）★ ●

10. When love relies on beauty, love disappears because of fading beauty.

（杨秀波 译）★

【93】水至清则无鱼，人至察则无徒。——戴德《大戴礼记》

投票：外方评委 7 人投票★，中方评委 12 人投票●

1. The water too clean feeds no fish, and the master too rigid breeds no disciple.

（艾朝阳 译）★ ★ ★ ● ● ● ●

2. No fish lives in water too clean; none follows one too discerning.

（叶如钢 译）★ ● ● ● ●

3. There would be no fish if the water is too pure; there would be no disciple if one is too strict.

（赖祎华 译）★ ★ ● ●

名言警句英译

4. Just as in water too limpid lives no fish, so a person too astute shall have no companion.

（张俊锋 译） ● ● ● ●

5. Extremity kills, moderation heals.

（冯雷 译） ★ ★ ●

6. Ultra-limpid water means no fish within; ultra-vigilant master means no follower after.

（王绍昌 译） ● ● ●

7. A creek too clear contains no fish; a man with eyes too sharp obtains no friends.

（铁冰 译 1） ● ● ●

8. If the water is too clear and pure, it will be difficult for fish to survive in it; if a person is too harsh to others, he will have no friends around him.

（倪庆行 译 1） ★ ●

9. A creek that can be seen through has no fish; a man who sees through everything has no friends.

（铁冰 译 2） ★ ●

10. Too pure water will have no fish; too shrewd a person will befriend nobody.

（倪庆行 译 2） ● ●

11. The water too pure is dangerous for fish; the person too exact is hostile to friends.

（曹小菁 译） ● ●

【94】凡事豫则立，不豫则废。——戴圣《礼记·中庸》

投票：外方评委7人投票★，中方评委5人投票●

1. If you fail to prepare, you prepare to fail.

（赖祎华 译，此译袭用 "By failing to prepare, you are preparing to fail." — Benjamin Franklin）★★★★★●

2. Whatever is prepared tends to succeed; whatever is unprepared leads to failure.

（曹小菁 译）★★●●●●

3. Under all circumstances, preparedness guarantees success; unpreparedness predicts failure.

（王绍昌 译1）★★●●●●

4. Preparation and planning ensures success; otherwise everything will end in a mess.

（张俊锋 译）★●●●

5. Preparation is the key to success.

（叶如钢 译）★★★★

6. Well planned, safe to land; jump at the call, a disastrous fall.

（冯雷 译）●●

7. Preparation is everything.

（艾朝阳 译，引自莎士比亚作品《哈姆雷特》）★

8. Be prepared! This is the key to success.

（王绍昌 译2）★

9. Success favours the prepared.

（乐国斌 译）★

【95】学然后知不足，教然后知困。——戴圣《礼记·学记》

投票：外方评委8人投票★，中方评委11人投票●

1. Study and then you'll know your lack of learning; teach and then you'll know your lack of understanding.

(赵宜忠 译) ★★★★●●●

2. Learning makes you know that you don't know it all; teaching makes you know where the difficulty lies.

(王昌玲 译) ★★★★★●●

3. Learning helps detect one's shortcomings, and teaching helps locate one's confusions.

(曹小菁 译) ●●●●●●●

4. It is learning that helps us see our own blindness; it is teaching that helps us feel others' puzzling.

(艾朝阳 译) ★★★★●

5. One learns and then needs to learn more, one teaches and then needs to understand better.

(叶如钢 译1) ★★★★●

6. The more you learn, the more certain you are that you have a lot to learn; the more you teach, the more certain you are that you have a lot to know.

(冯雷 译1) ★★★●●

7. When studying, you will know your lack of learning; when teaching, you will know the limitation of your knowledge.

(乐国斌 译) ★●●●●

8. Learning, one knows himself far from learned; teaching, one knows himself yet to be taught.

(铁冰 译) ●●●●●

9. It is through learning and teaching that we realize the lack of knowledge and skills.

（王绍昌 译1）★★●

10. In learning we see the need to learn more knowledge; in teaching, we find the importance of professional development.

（王绍昌 译2）●●●

11. Learn and know what you are wanting; teach and know where you are puzzled.

（石永浩 译）●●●

12. Learn and find more to learn; teach and find more to improve.

（王国己 译）★●

13. Learning and teaching help us grow.

（冯雷 译2）★●

14. A modest learner realizes more to learn on the road of pursuing knowledge. An attentive teacher discovers more to improve in the class instructing students.

（李开林 译）●●

15. Learn and then know lack of knowledge, teach and then see lack of understanding.

（叶如钢 译2）●●

16. The more I learn, the more I know I don't learn enough myself; the more I teach, the more I know I am not equipped with the abundant knowledge.

（任诚刚 译）●●

【96】一张一弛，文武之道也。——戴圣《礼记·杂记》

投票：外方评委3人投票★，中方评委4人投票●

1. Work and play, a balanced life.

（彭智鹏 译）★●●

2. A carrot and stick is the very trick.

（王昌玲 译）★●●

3. Work while you work and play while you play. This is the way to be happy and gay.

（张琼 译）★●

4. Engaged or relaxed? Better to be balanced.

（曹小菁 译）★●

5. Work and play, balance is best.

（杨秀波 译）★★

6. As Kings Wen and Wu govern well, one can't strain like hell.

（魏红霞 译）●●

7. Be tense and loose alternatively like a bow, following the great King Wen and King Wu.

（叶如钢 译）●●

8. Haste and rest, life balance at its best.

（王绍昌 译1）●●

9. To tense or to relax? To balance them is the best.

（石永浩 译）★

10. Should one perspire or just retire? Their combo one should admire and desire.

（王绍昌 译2）★

【97】傲不可长，欲不可纵，志不可满，乐不可极。

——戴圣《礼记·曲礼》

投票：外方评委7人投票★，中方评委5人投票●

1. Be it pride, desire, ambition or joy. Don't let it go wild, or it will destroy.

（王昌玲 译）★★★★★●●

2. Just as pride and desire should be caged so ambition and pleasure should be chained.

（石爱伟 译1）★●●●●●

3. Pride and desire must be kept within a moderate limit just as ambition and pleasure shouldn't be let to go unchecked.

（石爱伟 译2）★★★●●

4. Never let your pride grow, and bring your desire under control; keep your aspiration fresh as such, and enjoy pleasure but not too much.

（冯雷 译1）★★★●●

5. Go chase oats of life as you may; remember to control and check your way.

（王绍昌 译）●●●●●

6. Do not carry too far your pride, desires, ambition or pleasure.

（石永浩 译）★★★★

7. Never ever let go of your pride, joy, lust and ambition; things when reaching the extreme turn into the other direction.

（杨中仁 译）●●●●

8. Restless pride and indulgence as well as unreigned ambition and desire can be dangerous.

（艾朝阳 译）★★

名言警句英译

9. Contain your arrogance, rein your lust, harness your ambition and yoke your ecstasy—moderation counts.

（倪庆行 译）★★

10. Desire and pleasure should be reined, arrogance should die; when you reach the top, do not attempt to fly.

（冯雷 译2）●●

11. One can't let loose his arrogance or desire, nor can he go to extremes in his ambition or pleasure.

（魏红霞 译）★

【98】独学而无友，则孤陋而寡闻。——戴圣《礼记·学记》

投票：外方评委8人投票★，中方评委8人投票●

1. He who studies all by himself without peer discussion would become ig-norant and ill-informed.

（冯雷 译）★★★★★★★●●●●●●●●

2. Solitary learning without exchanging ideas with others will make one shallow-minded and ill-informed.

（王昌玲 译）★★★★★●●●●

3. If he learns without mate, one's knowledge can't be up to date.

（魏红霞 译）●●●●●

4. Aloof and detached, such a learner would be ignorant and poorly-in-formed.

（倪庆行 译）●●●●

5. Studying alone without friends makes a learner dull and ignorant.

（艾朝阳 译）●●●●

6. To study alone without a fellow makes one's knowledge narrow and sight shallow.

（张琼 译）●●●

7. To learn alone without others to communicate always narrows external sights and hinders free access to knowledge.

（郁序新 译）●●●

8. Self taught, bat blind.

（张晓阳 译）●●

9. On a lone path to learning without a companion one may end up with limited knowledge and scanty information.

（石爱伟 译）★

【99】曲高和寡，妙技难工。——阮瑀《筝赋》

投票：外方评委7人投票★，中方评委4人投票●

1. The highbrow music is less appreciated; the ingenious techniques are hard to master.

（何艳 译）★★★●

2. Arcane music finds fewer listeners; exquisite skills enjoy fewer artisans.

（董庆瑗 译）★★★●

3. The music is too highbrow to be popular; the skills are too superb for ordinary people to master.

（乐国斌 译）★★●●

4. Sophisticated melodies are played by few; superb skills are hard to master.

（叶如钢 译）★★●

5. Great music is hard to follow, and great skill is hard to master.

（马百亮 译）★★●

6. It's hard to echo elegant melody and master superb skills.

（董秀静 译）★●●

7. Highbrow songs find few singers; superb skills are hard to master.

（马建军 译）●●●

8. Highbrow songs find few singers; superb techniques find few masters.

（王毅 译，前半句借用）●●●

9. Highly sophisticated songs are difficult to sing; highly artistic skills are difficult to master.

（冯雷 译）★●

10. As your skill level goes up, the number of people that can enjoy goes down.

（陶家乐 译）★

11. Lofty celestial music finds little accordant notes.

（张俊锋 译）★

12. Difficult songs find few backup singers, and superb skills find few master hands.

（张晓阳 译）★

【100】 瓜田不纳履，李下不正冠。——曹植《君子行》

投票：外方评委 11 人投票★，中方评委 4 人投票●

1. In whatever circumstances, one should behave carefully to avoid unnecessary suspicion.

（杨中仁 译）★★★★★●●

2. To be reliable, never arouse suspicion.

（孙壮 译）★★★★★●

3. Don't do anything misleading to provoke suspicion.

（张立峰 译）★★★★★

4. Behave wisely and properly in the way that incurs no suspicion.

（王毅 译）★★★●

5. A highly-disciplined man does nothing that may put himself in a morally questionable situation.

（石爱伟 译）★●●

6. To avoid unnecessary misunderstanding or suspicion, don't bend to tie your shoes in a melon patch or fiddle with your cap under a plum tree.

（郁序新 译）★●●

7. A stranger bending down to tie his shoes in a melon field or raising his hand to adjust his hat in a plum orchard may well arouse the owner's suspicion of theft. A man of good manners should avoid such "innocent" gestures.

（冯雷 译）★●

8. Do your best to avoid suspicion on any occasion.

（张小琴 译）★★

9. Don't tie your shoelaces in a watermelon field or adjust your hat beneath a plum tree. Otherwise, people may suspect that you are a thief would-be.

（王昌玲 译）●●

10. Don't put on your shoes in a watermelon field; nor put right your cap under a plum tree. In other words, don't make yourself an easy target of being suspected.

（马金龙 译）●●

11. Don't carry your shoes when passing by a field of melon; don't extend your arms when passing under a tree of fruit. Untimely gestures would cause unnecessary suspicions.

（王梅兰 译）●●

12. To avoid being suspected, it's better not to bend yourself to wear your shoes by the watermelon field, and not to raise your hands to straighten your hat under the plum tree.

（艾朝阳 译）●●

13. To avoid arousing suspicion, stay away from taboo places.

（王成杰 译）★

14. Don't tie your shoelaces in a melon patch even if they're loosened or put your hat right under a plum tree even if it's askew.

（魏红霞 译）★

【101】 木秀于林，风必摧之；堆出于岸，流必湍之；行高于人，众必非之。

——李康《运命论》

投票：外方评委9人投票★，中方评委3人投票●

1. A tree that towers over others in the woods will be snapped by the wind; a mound that obtrudes from the shore will be scoured by the current; a person who excels will be maligned by jealous people.

（乐国斌 译）★ ★ ★ ●

2. Storms break higher trees. Waves erode protruding rocks. Criticisms fall on great minds.

（刘德江 译）★★●●

3. The tallest tree of the forest is shaken more by the wind; the earth nearest the bank is first swept away by the torrent; the man of high fame easily becomes a target of criticism.

（石爱伟 译）★●●

4. Those that stand out in the crowd are often crushed down first.

（王绍昌 译）★★★

5. As gales break giant oaks, and torrents wash away single mounds, so men slander sages.

（王成杰 译）★●

6. The tall trees in the forest are susceptible to damage by the windblow; the mound over the bank is prone to impact by the surging waves; the distinguished individuals are liable to discredit by their fellows.

（王毅 译）★●

7. Tall trees get knocked down by the wind; dirt piles above the shore get pounded by the waves; talented people get jealousy and hatred.

（陶家乐 译）★●

8. The tallest tree in woods is more breakable in gales. Rocky protrusions in river will be swept away by surging currents. A man of talents always invites envies from crowds.

（樊功生 译）●●

9. A tree that rises above others will be blown down by the wind; a mound that protrudes from the bank will be washed away by the current, and a person whose virtue is superior to that of others will be slandered.

（马百亮 译）★

10. Tall trees catch much wind; high achievers would attract much criticism.

（马建军 译）★

11. When a tree rises above the woods, the wind breaks it; when a mound of earth protrudes from the riverbank, the rapids wash it away; when a man is outstanding, he becomes the target of slander.

（冯雷 译）★

12. To stand out is to be the target to attack.

（杨胜悦 译）★

【102】志合者，不以山海为远，道乖者，不以咫尺为近。

——葛洪《抱朴子·博喻》

投票：外方评委 6 人投票★，中方评委 6 人投票●

1. Like minds meet, though oceans afar; stray minds wander, though feet apart.

（王绍昌 译）★★●●●

2. Distance can never set people of shared aspiration apart, nor can it bring people of differing principles near.

（王毅 译）★●●

3. Hearts in unison overcome the longest distance; opposed beliefs make the shortest distance far.

（叶如钢 译1）★●

4. When we are close at heart, mountains and oceans cannot keep us apart. When, with each other, we cannot see eye to eye, we will remain strangers, however hard we may try.

（马百亮 译1）★●

5. Mountains and seas are not obstacles for friends to get together; people of different principles don't visit each other even if they live in the same neighbourhood.

（石爱伟 译）★ ●

6. If we are of the same mind, we will be close even with mountains and oceans in between. If we are not of the same mind, however near we are, strangers we will remain.

（马百亮 译2）★ ●

7. Hobbies and ideas determine the distance between two persons.

（曹小菁 译）★ ●

8. Like-minded people will feel close even though they are separated by mountains and oceans; people who dislike each other may feel distant even if they are neighbors or families.

（董庆瑗 译）★ ★

9. For like-minded people, a long distance means nothing while for people with disagreements, a short distance seems two ends of the earth.

（董秀静 译）★ ★

10. No distance is long for the like-minded.

（王成杰 译）● ●

11. Adjacent values and desires transcend distance.

（陶家乐 译）● ●

12. With hearts in unison, we are close despite mountains and seas between us; with opposed beliefs, we are far apart even when physically close by.

（叶如钢 译2）★

【103】不饱食以终日，不弃功于寸阴。

——葛洪《抱朴子·勖学》

投票：外方评委8人投票★，中方评委3人投票●

1. Don't idle all day; make each moment count.

（王如利 译1）★★★●●

2. Don't spend every day just eating, don't waste a single moment of life.

（叶如钢 译）★★★

3. Don't be a well-fed idler and loaf all day; live each moment to its fullest while you may.

（王如利 译2）★●●

4. Don't just idle your days away on a full stomach. Seize every minute and try to do something meaningful.

（杨秀波 译）★★★

5. Don't idle away your time doing nothing meaningful because of laziness.

（董秀静 译）★●

6. Life is not about eating to fullness every day, but spending every minute in a meaningful way.

（吴春晓 译）★●

7. Never idle away by seeking satiety every day; do bring every minute into full play.

（倪庆行 译）●●

8. Don't be well-fed just to loaf about, but make every single moment count.

（乐国斌 译）●●

9. Don't just wine and dine all day long. Seize each minute to get things done.

（王昌玲 译）●●

10. Never be sated with delicious food, nor idle away your precious time.

（冯雷 译）★

11. Do not idle away your life with your stomach full. Do not waste any precious second at all!

（李少波 译）★

12. Neither eat or drink all day nor idle around doing nothing.

（郁序新 译）★

【104】奇文共欣赏，疑义相与析。

——陶渊明《移居二首·其一》

投票：外方评委11人投票★，中方评委4人投票●

1. Together we appreciate texts of the wise and clarify doubts as they arise.

（王绍昌 译）★★★★★★★★★★★●●●

2. Outstanding works we appreciate and share; doubtful points we exchange and analyze together.

（郁序新 译）★★★★★●●

3. Remarkable writings are recommended and appreciated by all; doubtful points are analyzed and discussed, big or small.

（冯雷 译）★●●●

4. Excellent articles we appreciate together, questionable points we discuss with one another.

（彭智鹏 译）●●●

5. Great essays are among my friends to share. Debates are done between us fair and square.

（石爱伟 译）●●

6. Marvelous articles for mutual appreciation; different opinions for collective discussion.

（曹小菁 译） ●●

7. Good articles are for us to appreciate and discriminate; when our opinions differ, we'd better confer.

（魏红霞 译） ★

8. It is a great pleasure for us to marvel at amazing articles and unravel puzzles together.

（倪庆行 译） ●

9. Excellent essays we share; all confusions we make clear.

（王昌玲 译） ●

【105】天下皆知取之为取，而莫知与之为取。

——范晔《后汉书·桓谭冯衍列传上》

投票：外方评委7人投票★，中方评委4人投票●

1. To take is to gain, which is known to all; but few know that the more you give, the more you'll gain.

（铁冰 译） ★★★★★★★●

2. All know to get is to take, few understand to give is to reap.

（杨秀波 译） ★★●●●

3. Most people think that to gain is to take, but few realize that to give is also to gain.

（艾朝阳 译） ★★●

4. The whole world regards taking as a gain without realizing giving is also a gain.

（王昌玲 译 1）●●●

5. We all know taking is to take, but not know giving is also to take.

（任诚刚 译 1）★●

6. Everyone knows that taking is obtaining, but may not realize that giving can also lead to obtaining.

（叶如钢 译 1）★★

7. The whole world see taking is gaining, but no one sees giving as another form of gaining.

（张俊锋 译）★★

8. We all know that to take is to take, but not know to give is also to take.

（任诚刚 译 2）●●

9. All know "taking" as "taking", but "giving" is also "taking" they know not.

（乐国斌 译）★

10. It's known to all that taking is a gain, yet none seems to know giving is a better gain.

（王昌玲 译 2）★

11. Everyone feels give is give and take is take; few realize give is also take, and give and take are integrated.

（冯雷 译）★

12. All men perceive gaining from others as taking literally, but not giving to others as taking conversely.

（魏红霞 译）★

13. Giving can be seeds for obtaining.

（叶如钢 译 2）★

【106】志士不饮盗泉之水，廉者不受嗟来之食。

——范晔《后汉书·列女传·乐羊子妻传》

投票：外方评委8人投票★，中方评委7人投票●

1. A man of noble character never drinks water from the "Stealing Spring" to quench his thirst, nor does he accept food handed out in contempt to satisfy his hunger.

（冯雷 译1）★★●●●●

2. A righteous man would rather die of thirst than drink water from a spring that bears a thief's name, would rather die of hunger than eat food handed out in contempt.

（倪庆行 译）★★●●●●

3. A man of integrity would rather die than drink or eat what is obtained against morality or propriety.

（石爱伟 译）★★★★●

4. People of integrity and virtue don't take alms. They have their honor and dignity.

（王昌玲 译）★★★★●

5. A gentleman would not drink stolen water; a clean hand would not take insulting food.

（彭智鹏 译）★●●●●

6. Even when he is thirsty, a man of integrity would still refuse to drink water obtained immorally; even when he is hungry, a man of dignity would still refuse to eat food offered to him insultingly.

（冯雷 译2）★★●

7. A person of integrity never drinks stolen water from other's well; a person of probity never takes Samaritan food offered as alms.

（王绍昌 译）●●●

8. A noble man would rather endure the torments of thirst and hunger than accept ill-gotten water nor rudely offered food.

(李开林 译) ●●●

9. A man of integrity does not drink stolen water, a man of dignity does not eat thrown food.

(杨中仁 译) ●●

10. A man of aspiration does not drink the water stolen from a spring; a man of integrity does not accept food from alms.

(赵宜忠 译) ●●

11. A noble man refuses stolen water; a fee beggar rejects insulting food.

(艾朝阳 译1) ●●

12. A man of spine does not condescend to get the spring water coming from the robber's garden; a beggar with sense of shame distains to accept the food from a man of contempt.

(艾朝阳 译2) ★

13. Dignified men neither drink water stolen from springs nor eat food begged from others.

(曹小菁 译) ★

第三篇
唐宋时期

Chapter III
Tang and Song Dynasties

【107】不忘故乡，仁也；不恋本土，达也。

——房玄龄《晋书·列传·第三章》

投票：外方评委8人投票★，中方评委6人投票●

1. A kind heart always embraces his hometown; a broad mind will never be tied down.

（樊功生 译）★★★★★●●●●

2. A hometown-bound heart is virtuous while a world-oriented mind is magnanimous.

（张俊锋 译）★★★●●●

3. Those who adore homeland are kind-hearted; those who go global are broad-minded.

（王绍昌 译）★●●

4. One bearing the hometown in mind is benevolent; one not confined to native land is liberal-minded.

（曹小菁 译）●●●

5. Those who are not indifferent to their home land are benevolent, and those who are not confined to their native land are broad-minded.

（王勍 译）★●

6. For a man of gentle heart, his home is home; for a man of open mind, his world is home.

（冯雷 译1）★●

7. A man who remembers his homeland is kind, and is free that his native land cannot bind.

（彭智鹏 译）●●

8. If your heart is kind, you will always keep your home in mind; if your mind is open, you do want to leave your home behind.

（冯雷 译2）●●

9. Bearing hometown in mind is a kind of benevolence, while leaving it for the distance is a kind of broadmindedness.

（张晔 译）●●

10. Keeping hometown in mind is a sign of being kind; happily parting with it mirrors a broad mind.

（石永浩 译1）●●

11. It is a kind man to be attached to his hometown; it is a wise man not to be confined to it.

（石永浩 译2）★

12. A kind man remembers his homeland for a good comfort and an open-minded man leaves his homeland for a better future.

（艾朝阳 译）★

【108】安危不贰其志，险易不革其心。

——魏征《群书治要·昌言》

投票：外方评委 10 人投票★，中方评委 5 人投票●

1. Perils won't change a perseverant mind, nor will hardship alter a determined heart.

（刘群 译）★★★★★★★●

2. Neither dangers nor difficulties can change original aspirations or make willing hearts waver.

（倪庆行 译，投票后修改）★★★★★●●

3. I will remain unswervingly committed to my mission even in the face of danger or risk.

（王毅 译）★★★●

4. Stay true to your ideals, be you in peace or crisis.

（王成杰 译）★●●

5. In peace or in perils, stick to your initial inspirations.

（王绍昌 译）★●●

6. In safety or danger, never waver in your resolve. In prosperity or adversity, never betray your heart.

（王如利 译）●●●

7. Whether the situation is safe or dangerous, whether it is easy or difficult to carry out one's plan, one should not give up his original aspiration and personal integrity.

（董秀静 译）★●

8. Be resolute whether it's safe or dangerous, easy or difficult.

（曹小菁 译）★★

9. Neither peril nor peace can make our aspirations change or cease.

（冯雷 译）●●

10. A brave heart won't be destroyed by hardships and shaken by dangers.

（张晔 译）★

11. Don't change your ambition in times of crisis, and don't yield to the environment in times of danger.

（邢琏 译）★

【109】疾风知劲草，板荡识诚臣。——李世民《赐萧瑀》

投票：外方评委9人投票★，中方评委5人投票●

1. Strong grasses survive in rough winds; loyal men thrive in tough times.

（崔传明 译）★★●

2. Hard times try man's soul as rough winds test the toughness of grass.

（吴春晓 译）★ ●

3. Just as resilient grass holds its ground in high winds, loyal officials stand firm in turbulent times.

（冯雷 译）★ ●

4. Turmoil tests loyalty as gales tell sturdiness.

（田璐 译）★ ●

5. High winds show tough grasses; hard times true patriots.

（刘向军 译）★ ★

6. Turmoil tests the loyal just as strong wind tests tough grass.

（魏红霞 译）★ ★

7. As strong winds reveal the toughness of grass, hard times test the loyalty of officials.

（石永浩 译）★ ★

8. Tough wind reveals strong grass; hard times tell loyal officials.

（曹小菁 译）★ ★

9. The fierce wind can tell whether a blade of grass is tensile or fragile just as troubled times can tell whether a minister is loyal or vile.

（倪庆行 译）● ●

10. As sturdy grass withstands high winds, a loyal man perseveres in the midst of turmoil.

（马建军 译）★

【110】相知无远近，万里尚为邻。

——张九龄《送韦城李少府》

投票：外方评委7人投票★，中方评委9人投票●

1. The distance cannot set us apart as long as we are close in heart.

（张琼 译）★ ★ ★ ★ ★ ● ● ● ● ● ●

2. Distance makes no difference for us bosom friends. Ten thousand miles apart, we can still feel each other's beating heart.

（王毅 译）★ ★ ★ ★ ★ ★

3. Friendship never suffers from the distance; miles apart or next-door makes no difference.

（石永浩 译）★ ★ ● ● ●

4. True friends, even with a world apart, feel as close as neighbors.

（倪庆行 译）★ ★ ● ●

5. Far or near, sincere friendship doesn't care; thousands of miles away or even more, seems just next door.

（张晓阳 译）★ ★ ● ●

6. Our genuine friendship shall transcend space. Though oceans apart, we seem face to face.

（王昌玲 译1）● ● ● ●

7. Far or near, we know each other; miles apart, we feel like neighbor.

（魏红霞 译）● ● ● ●

8. A genuine bond knows no distance, a faraway pal could still feel next-door.

（樊功生 译）● ● ●

9. Distance is never for true friendship a barrier, a thousand miles doesn't stop us feeling as close as ever.

（石爱伟 译）● ● ●

名言警句英译

10. No matter how far apart, always near is a soul mate's heart.

（杨秀波 译）●●●

11. Long distance cannot stop true friendship from growing.

（冯雷 译）★●

12. My friend, even miles apart, you are close to my heart.

（王昌玲 译2）●●

13. Bosom friends will not mind whether they live close or far apart; even physically thousands of miles apart, they will feel they are neighbours in their hearts.

（段冰知 译）★

14. Distance draws friends near and makes friends dear.

（陈赛花 译）★

【111】老当益壮，宁移白首之心? 穷且益坚，不坠青云之志。

——王勃《滕王阁序》

投票：外方评委8人投票★，中方评委6人投票●

1. Aging won't wear out my heart; hardships only strengthen my mind.

（冯雷 译）★★★●●

2. Poverty and old age are no excuse for leading a worthless life.

（刘向军 译）★★★★★

3. Years may wrinkle my skin but never my soul; tough situation only toughens me to hold up my lofty ideal.

（王毅 译）●●●●●

4. Never give up your lofty ideals and aspirations, even in old age or adversity.

（石永浩 译）★★●●

5. Old as I am, I should be more ambitious, how can I change my ideal when my hair turns grey. Poor as I am, I should be more unyielding, and I'll adhere to my ambition and never give up.

（张晓阳 译）●●●

6. Old age should only make one stand firmer in a lifelong pursuit, not waver; likewise, poverty should boost one's aspiration, not undermine it.

（吴春晓 译）★●

7. Old but still ambitious, never let age change your heart; poor but rather tough, never let poverty block your dream.

（董庆瑗 译）★●

8. Old age and poverty should be more of a stimulus than a hindrance to one's lofty aspirations.

（叶步青 译）●●

9. Our minds get stronger as we age. Either at an old age or in poverty, we should never give up our ambitious pursuits.

（王梅兰 译）★

10. My determination get stronger as I grow old, my ambition never decline as I am in difficult situation.

（张立国 译）★

11. Though old and stuck in adversity, I won't betray my principle or abandon my ambition.

（王昌玲 译）★

12. When hale and poor, remain hearty and potent.

（王绍昌 译,部分借用英语谚语）★

名言警句英译

【112】独在异乡为异客，每逢佳节倍思亲。

——王维《九月九日忆山东兄弟》

投票：外方评委7人投票★，中方评委9人投票●

1. Alone as a resident where I don't truly belong, on every festive day my yearning for home grows strong.

（冯雷 译1）★★★★★●●●●●●●●

2. Away and alone from home for years I wander, each special day makes my love of being home grow fonder.

（冯雷 译2）●●●●●●●●

3. Alone, a stranger in a strange land I now dwell; on festive days longing for kinfolk I can't quell.

（石永浩 译）★●●●●●●

4. As a stranger in the alien land far away, I am aye doubly homesick every festive day.

（赵宜忠 译）★●●●●●

5. On festive day, in alien land lonely, I so much more miss my family.

（叶如钢 译）●●●●

6. Alone as a stranger in a strange place, I'm homesick manyfold on festive days.

（刘群 译）★★●

7. A wayfarer alone, from hometown far away, I'm even more nostalgic on a festive day.

（铁冰 译）★●●

8. Alone in a remote place, I'm a lonely guest, whenever on festivals, I miss my home deepest.

（张琼 译）★●

9. Every time a festival arrives I couldn't help crying, as I'm so lonely a stranger to the foreign land. I miss my parents two times as far as I'm away from my homeland.

（艾朝阳 译1）●●

10. I feel so lonely here as a stranger to the houses, missing my parents there in my hometown. I feel lonely more whenever a festival arrives, missing both my parents and my homeland.

（艾朝阳 译2）★

【113】天生我材必有用，千金散尽还复来。

——李白《将进酒》

投票：外方评委11人投票★，中方评委7人投票●

1. I believe I was born with the ability to achieve, and what I give I will certainly receive.

（冯雷 译1）★★★★★★★★★★●●●●

2. Everyone living in the world will play a role, greater or lesser; gold given away will be earned back, sooner or later.

（石永浩 译1）★★★★★★●●●

3. I was born for a certain reason, time will come for me to complete my mission; I never mind giving money away, for I know the principle of earning and pay.

（冯雷 译2）★★★★●●●●

4. Any man is born to be a talent in some way; gold coins gone will be regained someday.

（石永浩 译2）★●●●●●

名言警句英译

5. My talent blessed by Heaven not in vain; myriad of gold coins, if gone, come again.

(叶如钢 译) ●●●

6. My heaven-endowed talents will be displayed for certain; gold coins galore gone will be gained again.

(倪庆行 译) ●●●

7. Gifted am I, destined as Heaven sent: thousands of gold coins, once gone, will again ascend.

(王绍昌 译) ★●

8. (When in pride, enjoy to the full our life's delight; never leave your cup unfilled under the moon bright!) Remember, we were born a gifted, worthy brain, and however much spent, our gold shall come back again.

(铁冰 译) ★●

9. God existing in me will surely help prove my talent; likewise, pennies are spent but dollars will surely be earned back.

(曹小菁 译) ★●

10. My heaven-sent talent's destined for sensation. Tons of gold squandered is easily re-obtained.

(王昌玲 译) ●●

11. My innate talent will be in use, lots of treasure lost will be retrieved.

(杨秀波 译) ●●

12. Useful will be my talents endowed and innate; retrievable will be my lost riches sooner or late.

(程永生 译) ●●

13. As Gift of God, I'm somewhat gifted for some accomplishments with all spent golds repaid.

(艾朝阳 译1) ★

14. I believe in God's power in me who can be somebody someday with all repayment due.

（艾朝阳 译2） ★

15. The powers which heaven has wrought to me must have had a purpose; thousands of gold can be earned and spent again.

（任诚刚 译） ★

【114】 清水出芙蓉，天然去雕饰。
——李白《经乱离后天恩流夜郎忆旧游书怀赠江夏韦太守良宰》

投票：外方评委 10 人投票★，中方评委 6 人投票●

1. Artificial beauty is never equal to that of pure nature.

（石爱伟 译） ★★★★★★★

2. From clear water is a lotus flower, being endowed with beauty of nature.

（杨秀波 译） ●●●●●

3. Out of clear water lotus stands there, it's so naturally elegant and fair.

（叶如钢 译1） ★●●●

4. (Literary works should be) like the lotus flower that just comes out of clear water, beautiful and bright as created purely by nature.

（冯雷 译1） ★★★★

5. A good article is natural and fresh as the lotus out of clear water.

（张琼 译） ●●●●

6. You are so charming, my darling, like the bathing lily flower standing out of the clear water, undecorated and pure.

（艾朝阳 译） ★★●

7. Fresh bathed out of the clear water, the lotus charms with natural color.

（张俊锋 译）★★●

8. Lotus comes out of clear water, ornament creations are done by nature wright.

（任诚刚 译）●●●

9. Above clear water, lotus flowers look gorgeous and elegant; it can only be the nature that makes them eminent.

（冯雷 译2）●●●

10. From clear water, lilies are the purest; naturally graced, they stand above the rest.

（王绍昌 译）★★

11. From water lotus is blooming, which is plain and without grooming.

（魏红霞 译）●●

12. The lotus out of clear water is so natural that is far beyond hand-made.

（杨中仁 译）●●

13. Risen out of clear water, lotus' beauty is from nature.

（叶如钢 译2）●●

第三篇　唐宋时期

【115】天不言而四时行，地不语而百物生。

——李白《上安州裴长史书》

投票：外方评委8人投票★，中方评委6人投票●

1. The sky says nothing yet four seasons flow; the earth says nothing yet all plants grow.

（华卫 译）★★★●●●●●

2. Seasons change and lives flourish despite no word from heaven or earth.

(樊功生 译) ★★★●●

3. Wordless, the skies witness four seasons come and go; speechless, the earth sees various beings grow.

(石永浩 译1) ★●●●

4. Though Heaven's silent, seasons flow; while Earth stays quiet, all flora grow.

(叶如钢 译) ●●●●

5. Everything has its own law.

(丁如伟 译) ★★●

6. Nature has its laws.

(王成杰 译1) ★★★

7. With seasons alternating in due course, nature nurtures creatures without words.

(倪庆行 译) ●●●

8. The sky is silent, yet four seasons rotate. The earth is silent, yet all living things proliferate.

(王昌玲 译) ●●●

9. The four seasons rotate as usual though the sky does not utter; all things grow even the earth does not order.

(任诚刚 译1) ●●●

10. Heaven speaks not, but four seasons change orderly; earth dictates not, but all creatures grow vibrantly.

(王毅 译1) ★●

11. Heaven speaks no words, but it can make four seasons rotate; earth speaks no words, but it can make all living things grow.

(张晓阳 译1) ★●

12. Who says heaven has no words? It speaks through the rotation of four seasons. Who says earth has no words? It speaks through the growth of all living things.

(张晓阳 译2) ★●

13. Silent are the earth and heaven, yet beings grow in each season.

(石永浩 译2) ●●

14. Silence is better than sound.

(任诚刚 译2) ★

15. Nature is wordless. However, seasons change and all things grow.

(王成杰 译2) ★

16. Nature works not as man wishes.

(王婷 译) ★

17. Without announcement the four seasons cycle; in silence all creatures grow.

(李慧 译) ★

18. Inaction is the best action: while Heaven and Earth dictate not, seasons and all creatures run orderly in their own course.

(王毅 译2) ★

19. The best thing one can do when it's raining is to let it rain.

(郁序新 译, 借用 Henry Wadsworth Longfellow) ★

【116】吾观自古贤达人，功成不退皆殒身。

——李白《行路难·其三》

投票：外方评委7人投票★，中方评委6人投票●

1. I have noticed a fact in history that a great person would meet his downfall if he did not retire after his great achievement.

（杨秀波 译）★★●●●●

2. My observations of the sages tell me that those who refused to retreat after being crowned with success all inevitably perished.

（王梅兰 译）★★●●●

3. The talents who win glory but fail to retire have all ended up with tragedy.

（王成杰 译）★●●●

4. Of all saints and sages of yore, none's free from misfortune at all.

（王昌玲 译）★●●

5. By observing the wise men of the past, they will die of unnatural causes if they do not retire after recognition and success.

（陶家乐 译）★★★

6. All those who finished their mission and did not choose to retire, eventually fell victim to their own unwise desire.

（冯雷 译）★●

7. Talented and celebrated men from ancient times, as I see it, all end up tragically if they do not resign at the peak of success.

（何艳 译）★●

8. Wise courtiers should retire timely with success, or unexpected persecutions would be waiting ahead.

（张莹 译）●●

9. It is my observation that every prominent personage who had refused to retire after achieving great feats died an untimely death since ancient times.

（倪庆行 译）★

10. In ancient times, only those who chose to retire before reaching the height in politics were wise enough to survive all schemes.

（石永浩 译）★

【117】 出师未捷身先死，长使英雄泪满襟。——杜甫《蜀相》

投票：外方评委8人投票★，中方评委6人投票●

1. You had devoted heart and soul to the fruitless expeditions for years; your unexpected death moved later men of ambition to countless tears.

（冯雷 译）★●●●●●●

2. You passed away before the win it is so mournful; all heroes take off hats to you, running tears painful.

（郁序新 译）★●●●●

3. How tragic it is for the hero to die without fulfilling his ambition.

（艾朝阳 译）★★★★

4. His ambition unfulfilled he in the battlefront died, many with heroic spirits have for his untimely death sighed.

（石爱伟 译）★★●

5. You fight and fall down before the cheer; millions of people are saddened in tears.

（张琼 译）●●●

6. Before the final win, thou decease; later heroes shed tears hard to cease.

（王昌玲 译）●●●

7. Your untimely passing in a war, premier, brings heroic men to constant tears.

（樊功生 译）★★

8. He led to conquer the enemy and died when victory was near, which has brought heroes after heroes to many a tear.

（叶如钢 译1）★★

9. He passed away prior to the decisive victory, which often makes succeeding heroes wet their sleeves with hot tears.

（倪庆行 译）●●

10. He died sans victory to reap, for which so many heroes weep.

（石永浩 译）●●

11. You passed away, before claiming the final victory, in prime; deeply moved, heroes shed tears sublime.

（王绍昌 译）●●

12. The great Zhuge died before conquering the enemy, and heroes after heroes sigh for the tragic fate.

（叶如钢 译2）●●

13. He died before his army won the war despite his devotion and desire. Countless heroes shed tears for his broken dream.

（杨秀波 译）●●

14. Sacrifice before achieving triumph in battle always makes heroes sorrowful and tearful.

（张晓阳 译）★

【118】读书破万卷，下笔如有神。

——杜甫《奉赠韦左丞丈二十二韵》

投票：外方评委10人投票★，中方评委15人投票●

1. Ample reading breeds gifted writing.

（刘群 译）★★★●●●●●●

2. He who reads extensively writes beautifully.

（王琳 译）★★★●●●●

3. Widely read, wisely write.

（冯雷 译1）★●●●●●●●

4. Bookworm for many a year, sharp-penned as Shakespeare.

（冯雷 译2）●●●●●●●●

5. Excellent writing stems from extensive reading.

（华卫 译1）★★★●●●

6. Extensive reading empowers writing.

（王如利 译）★★★●●

7. Read over thousands of books, ideas flow down like brooks.

（徐艺玮 译1）●●●●

8. Extensive reading helps one's thoughts drip out of his pen.

（王昌玲 译1）★★●

9. Well read, well expressed.

（王昌玲 译2）★●●

10. Read widely and well, and you'll pour your brilliant thoughts out of pen as if from a magical spell.

（倪庆行 译）★●●

11. An expressive writer is first an erudite reader.

（许霖越 译）★●●

12. Read like a dog, write like a god.

（陈良 译）●●●

13. Read extensively, write fluently.

（徐艺玮 译2）★●

14. He who is a voracious reader is a gifted writer.

（陈光华 译）★●

15. Reading abundantly makes one write fluently.

（曹小菁 译）★●

16. Extensive reading enables one to write as if with God's help.

（华卫 译2）●●

17. Widely reading, smoothly writing.

（孟朝岗 译）●●

18. The God rewards the magic pen to those well-read.

（魏建国 译）●●

19. Write fluently as inspired by God after reading through thousands of books.

（彭智鹏 译）●●

20. Read a million, beat Lord Byron.

（刘亚木 译）●●

21. Reading abounds, writing blossoms.

（徐英才 译）★

名言警句英译

【119】文章千古事，得失寸心知。——杜甫《偶题》

投票：外方评委7人投票★，中方评委4人投票●

1. Writing transcends time, but the feeling is only experienced by the author.

(陶家乐 译) ★★★★

2. Aimed to go down for a thousand years, writing is a grave affair; of its sweetness and bitterness, only the writer is aware.

(石永浩 译) ★★★

3. Writing is meant to transcend time and place. Only authors know what challenge to face.

(王昌玲 译) ●●●

4. Writing is such a never-ending business; only the writer knows the ups-and-downs about it.

(孙玲玲 译) ★●

5. No masterminds, no masterworks.

(刘向军 译) ★●

6. Poems and essays live through the ages, and the gains and losses reside in the hearts of the authors.

(田璐 译) ★★

7. A writer is never too fond of the sound of his own voice.

(叶步青 译) ★★

8. Only the author of a masterpiece knows what it takes to make it perpetual.

(王梅兰 译) ●●

9. An excellent article is something which spreads through the ages, only the writer himself knows best about the gain and loss behind.

(张晓阳 译) ●●

10. Whether poetry and prose will be handed down to generations to come, it is their authors that are most aware of the gains and losses in creation.

(倪庆行 译) ● ●

11. Good articles will pass down for centuries, but only the authors themselves know the gains and hardships.

(魏红霞 译) ● ●

12. Time tries a work, but the writer knows it.

(王成杰 译) ★

13. A great writer reflects on both the merits and flaws in his writing, as he believes great literature endures through time.

(李开林 译) ★

14. Literary writing matters throughout the ages. No one but the writer knows its joys and sorrows.

(丁如伟 译) ★

【120】朱门酒肉臭，路有冻死骨。

——杜甫《自京赴奉先县咏怀五百字》

投票：外方评委4人投票★，中方评委4人投票●

1. The rich binge on meat; the poor starve on street.

(崔传明 译) ★ ★ ★

2. While the leftovers of the rich spoil, the poor freeze to death in the streets.

(王成杰 译) ★ ●

3. Meat goes bad in the houses of the rich, but some starve to death on the road.

（杨秀波 译）★★

4. Inside the vermilion gate, wine turns sour and meat smells rotten, while outside the gate lie the bones of the starved and the frozen.

（张晓阳 译）●●

5. Behind the vermilion gates, the leftover meat and wine are smelly; on the roadside, there're bones of those who die from cold and hunger.

（魏红霞 译）●●

6. The rich let surplus food rot at home while the poor suffer from hunger.

（何冰 译）★

7. While wine and meat may stink inside red gates, frozen bodies are strewn along pathways.

（倪庆行 译）●

8. The wine and meat stink at landlord's house, but there are frozen bones on the road.

（任诚刚 译）●

9. The rich did not mind seeing meat rotten, while the poor either got starved or frozen.

（石永浩 译）●

10. Whereas meat and wine are thrown away from vermillion gates with pride, the poor are dying of hunger and cold at roadside.

（王绍昌 译）●

11. While the rich leave meat untouched and wine untried, the poor are frozen to death on the roadside.

（刘雪芹 译）●

12. The rich wine and dine, while the poor die of cold and hunger by the roadside.

（马建军 译）●

13. The rich turn meat and wine into waste. The poor dead from hungry at cold street.

（张立国 译）●

14. From behind the red door, wafts the fragrance of meat and wine. Along the road, lie the starved people who turn to white bones.

（王昌玲 译）●

15. The smells of wines and meats are wafted out from the red mansion of the rich, while the corpses died of hunger are still seen on the roadside. (It's a scene described in an ancient poem.)

（杨中仁 译）●

16. Wealthy household smells the aroma of meat and whine, while bones of people starved to death scatter outdoors.

（曹小菁 译）●

【121】宽心应是酒，遣兴莫过诗。——杜甫《可惜》

投票：外方评委6人投票★，中方评委4人投票●

1. Wine is the best relief for my heart; poetry is the best diversion for the mind.

（吴春晓 译）★★★●

2. While wine is most soothing, poetry is most entertaining.

（乐国斌 译）★●●

3. One can either drown his sorrow in wine, or find the best outlet through poetry.

（王如利 译）★★★

名言警句英译

4. Wine soothes the soul and poetry raises the spirits.

（冯雷 译）●●●

5. Wine soothes your heart and poetry lightens it.

（王慧玉 译）★●

6. To relieve anxiety we drink liquor, to dispel sorrow we write poetry.

（何艳 译）★★

7. What can soothe my heart is but wine. What can vent my feelings is but poems.

（王毅 译）●●

8. From wine I get relief; from poetry I get pleasure.

（王成杰 译）★

9. Drink some wine to let loose a bit, read poems to be more educated and happy.

（陶家乐 译）★

【122】师者，所以传道受业解惑也。——韩愈《师说》

投票：外方评委11人投票★，中方评委13人投票●

1. A teacher enlightens minds, imparts knowledge and answers doubts.

（张琼 译）★★★★★★★★★★★●●●●●●●●●

2. A teacher is an enlightener, mentor and visioner.

（王昌玲 译1）★★●●●●●●●●●

3. A teacher is a life guide, knowledge interpreter, skill trainer and wisdom enlightener.

（冯雷 译1）●●●●●●●●

4. A qualified teacher teaches his students life philosophy, imparts professional knowledge and skills to them and clears up their confusions.

(冯雷 译2) ★●●●●

5. A teacher is to teach, to enable, and to enlighten.

(曹小菁 译) ★●●●●

6. The teacher is he who brings enlightenment, reason and vision to the human mind.

(王昌玲 译2) ★●●●

7. The teacher can be a channel for knowledge, a master for apprentice, and a fixer for perplexes.

(艾朝阳 译1) ●●●●

8. A teacher is a communicator, a mentor, and an instructor.

(王绍昌 译1) ★★●

9. A teacher propagates doctrines, imparts knowledge and resolves doubts.

(王绍昌 译2) ●●

10. Teachers are those who preach truth, teach technique and dispel confusion.

(华卫 译) ●●

11. A teacher uncovers truth, transduces knowledge, prebuilds professions, and fixes perplexities.

(艾朝阳 译2) ●●

12. Teachers are those who enlighten the human mind, train people skills and explain how and why things happen.

(魏建国 译) ★

【123】业精于勤，荒于嬉；行成于思，毁于随。

——韩愈《进学解》

投票：外方评委 3 人投票★，中方评委 3 人投票●

1. Learning excels due to diligence and collapses due to indulgence. Actions succeed due to thoughtfulness and fail due to carelessness.

（叶如钢 译）★●

2. Achievements are reached by hard work rather than recreation. Actions are done after thorough consideration rather than casual decision.

（任诚刚 译1）★

3. An art is perfected by frequent practice and deserted by disaffection; an achievement is made by thoughtful polish and destroyed by rashness.

（艾朝阳 译1）★

4. One's career is made because of diligence, ruined of slack; success begins with thought and ends with casual action.

（任诚刚 译2）●

5. Learning hard, you'll ace; playing truant, you'll fail. Thinking independently, you'll succeed; following the herd, you'll achieve nothing.

（铁冰 译）●

6. Knowledge increases with diligence and decreases with layabout; a decision results with thoughtfulness and fails with rush.

（艾朝阳 译2）●

7. Study is improved through diligence and worsened through negligence. Conduct is bettered through reflection and ruined by conformity.

（王昌玲 译）●

8. Diligence enhances academic proficiency and playfulness ruins it; reflection promotes conduct and casualty shatters it.

（冯雷 译）●

【124】 世有伯乐，然后有千里马，千里马常有，而伯乐不常有。

——韩愈《马说》

投票：外方评委6人投票★，中方评委11人投票●

1. Which horse runs fast and far? The answer is with Bole the star. He was an expert on horses, the best of the best judges. Superior horses are not rare, how to find Bole is what we care. Talents look common without doubt, only keen eyes can sort them out.

（冯雷 译）★★●●●●●●●●

2. The steed spotter can tell which horse can gallop a thousand miles. Yet, it will take a blue moon for a superb gallant horse to encounter such a spotter.

（倪庆行 译）★★★★●●●●

3. The first genius might not be regarded as a "genius" only when there comes a pair of sharp eyes that can distinguish him. What our world really lacks is not talented people but the eyes to single them out.

（李开林 译）★●●●●

4. Talent scouts come before talents; talents abound but talent scouts are rarely found.

（乐国斌 译1）●●●●●

5. Master connoisseurs come before far galloping horses. Far galloping horses are everywhere, but Master connoisseurs are rarely seen.

（王绍昌 译）★●●●

6. There is Master Bole, and then thousand-mile horses are recognized. Thousand-mile horses are often around, but Boles are rare.

（叶如钢 译）●●●

7. In the world there's Bole first, then a swift horse. A swift horse is often available, but Bole is not always available.

(赵宜忠 译) ●●●

8. It takes talent scouts to discover talents; but there are more talents than scouts.

(王昌玲 译) ★★

9. Only by a good finder can a good horse be singled out. However, there are excellent horses oftentimes without their finders.

(铁冰 译) ★●

10. There's a man named Bole in the world first and then a thousand-li horse. A thousand-li horse is easily found, but Bole is not found often.

(任诚刚 译) ●●

11. Only Bo'le the master has distinguished the horse superior; there're always horses superior while Bo'les are rare.

(魏红霞 译) ●●

12. Horse connoisseurs pave the way for swift horses; compared to swift horses, horse connoisseurs are more of rarity.

(乐国斌 译2) ★

13. Since Bo'le comes to our world, we know which horse can gallop thousands of miles. It is not difficult to find such horses, but it is difficult to come across such a person like Bo'le.

(程永生 译) ★

【125】是故弟子不必不如师，师不必贤于弟子，闻道有先后，术业有专攻，如是而已。

——韩愈《师说》

投票：外方评委9人投票★，中方评委5人投票●

1. Nobody can be an expert in everything. Teachers themselves are just learners earlier than students. Therefore, students may outdo their teachers and teachers may be surpassed by their students.

（铁冰 译）★★★★★★★★★●●

2. Actually, an apprentice may not always be less skilled than his master, and the master may not always be more worthy than his apprentice. Knowledge can be acquired at a different time, and skill can be specialized. That's all there to it.

（樊功生 译）★★★●●●●

3. Therefore, pupils are not necessarily inferior to their master, but it is at different times that they are enlightened and in different fields that they specialize; that's it.

（张俊锋 译）★★●●●●●

4. Teachers are not necessarily more virtuous and capable than their students and students are not destined to be inferior. It is only that teachers were educated earlier. Strength and success in a special field depends on industry and inspiration, on nothing else.

（石爱伟 译）●●●●●

5. Therefore, students are not necessarily academically inferior to teachers; teachers are not guaranteed more virtuous than students. Learning takes place at varied times, earlier or later; students and teachers can both be specialized in one way or another. That's the way with learning.

（王绍昌 译）●●●●●

名言警句英译

6. In fact, students are not necessarily inferior to their teacher. The teacher is not always superior to his students. Put it simply, it is equally applicable for anyone, teachers or students, that there is a specialization in knowledge and skills and a sequence of acquiring the truth.

（冯雷 译）★★●

7. The disciples needn't always be inferior to their master, who needn't always be superior to his disciples. People get enlightened at different time and have different fortes, that's all.

（王昌玲 译）●●●

8. Thus a student needs not be inferior to the teacher, and a teacher needs not be more virtuous than the students. Knowledge is acquired by one before another, and we specialize in different subjects. That's all.

（叶如钢 译）●

9. A student is not necessarily inferior to his teacher while a teacher may not outshine his students. Because the teacher just learn earlier and everyone has his own field he is good at. A master of a profession lies not time, but something else.

（杨秀波 译）●

10. When we start learning and where we specialize differ from person to person. Therefore, it is natural that a student may outshine his teacher some way.

（石永浩 译）●

【126】文章合为时而著，歌诗合为事而作。

——白居易《与元九书》

投票：外方评委7人投票★，中方评委17人投票●

1. Articles are what their eras provoke; poems are what specific events evoke.

（倪庆行 译）★★★★★★●●●●●●●●●

2. Essays and proses are yells of the roles; songs and poems are cries of the souls.

（冯雷 译1）●●●●●●●

3. Articles are written at the call of the time; poems are composed for the need of life.

（王绍昌 译1）★★●●●●

4. Articles reflect time, while poems sing life.

（王绍昌 译2）★★★●●

5. Articles should reflect the characteristics of time, while poetry should reflect the characteristics of life.

（魏红霞 译）★★●●●

6. Writers write for their time; poets sing for their life.

（冯雷 译2）★●●●●

7. A good article fits the time well and a good poem rhymes the event well.

（艾朝阳 译1）★●●●

8. Articles present times; poems depict life.

（田霞 译）●●●●

9. Writers present time; poets eulogize life.

（王绍昌 译3）★●●

10. For life, the writer offers prose; for love, the poet presents rose.

（冯雷 译3）★●●

11. A good article rides a horse of tide, and a good poem touches the soul of time.

（艾朝阳 译2） ●●●

12. Prose and poetry are composed for the spirit of the time.

（王昌玲 译） ★●

13. Articles should be written for the times, poetry for people's lives.

（张琼 译） ★●

14. While articles are written by request of times, poems are composed in light of events.

（许霖越 译） ●●

【127】在天愿作比翼鸟，在地愿为连理枝。

——白居易《长恨歌》

投票：外方评委3人投票★，中方评委8人投票●

1. In heaven we would like to be two birds flying together, and on earth two trees with branches interlocked forever.

（任诚刚 译） ★★●●●●

2. Like birds we fly in unison, joining our forces of wing and foot; like trees we thrive as one, combining our vigor of twig and root.

（叶如钢 译1） ●●●●

3. If only we were forever interlocked, like two birds flying wing to wing in sky and two trees with branches twined on earth.

（王绍昌 译） ★★●

4. We would never part, either as birds flying together or vines twined forever.

（石永浩 译） ●●●

5. May we become birds of love in the sky! May we be twin trees growing into one!

（王昌玲 译）●●●

6. In the sky, we'd like to be two lovebirds free, and on the earth twinned branches of a tree.

（赵宜忠 译）●●●

7. Let us be two birds soaring in the sky together, and two trees intertwined on earth forever.

（倪庆行 译）★●

8. Up in the sky, I'd be your wings; down on the earth, you'd be my roots.

（刘群 译）●●

9. In the sky, like lovebirds wing next to wing together; on earth, like twin trees twig holding twig forever.

（叶如钢 译2）★

10. Let us have one wing each flying in pairs in the sky; let us be two branches of one tree growing on the earth.

（李开林 译）★

【128】 莫笑贱贫夸富贵，共成枯骨两如何？

——白居易《放言五首·其四》

投票：外方评委 14 人投票★，中方评委 4 人投票●

1. Stop acting like a snob. Rich or not, all are bound to die.

（刘向军 译）★★★★★★●●

2. Neither mock the poor nor flatter the rich; all will end up buried deep in the ditch.

（王昌玲 译）★★★★●

3. Neither despise the humble nor flatter the noble, as both of their skeletons resemble.

（崔传明 译）★★★★

4. Don't admire rich and distain poor. Everything will turn into earth regardless of rich or poor.

（张立国 译）★★★★

5. Laugh not at the poor. When has death ever spared the rich?

（石永浩 译）★★●●

6. Whether rich or poor, it matters not; are we not all equal in death, bones and rot?

（杨胜悦 译）★●●●

7. Death is equal to the rich and the poor. Don't despise the poor and show off your wealth.

（郁序新 译）★●●

8. Don't despise the poor and low, or admire the rich and high, for all are equal after we die.

（冯雷 译）★★

9. Never despise the poor or value the rich for all will turn out to be skeleton in the end.

（杨秀波 译）★★

10. Don't insult those who are poor and chase after those who are rich; after all, they all look the same when dead.

（陶家乐 译）★●

11. Could the rich still flaunt their wealth before the poor when both are dry skeletons?

（吴春晓 译）★

12. Laud not the prince, disdain not the pauper: rotten bones they both ultimately become. Where then are the people?

（王绍昌 译）★

13. Don't brag your wealth and tease others' poverty. After death, to their grave no one can take a penny.

（董庆瑗 译）★

14. No matter rich or poor, honoured or lowly, after death, whose bone doesn't decay?

（杨中仁 译）★

【129】 我生本无乡，心安是归处。——白居易《初出城留别》

投票：外方评委7人投票★，中方评委5人投票●

1. Home is where my heart is.

（王绍昌 译）★★★●●●

2. Home is where my heart belongs, rather than where I was first born.

（石爱伟 译）★★★●

3. I have no hometown other than where my heart is consoled.

（曹小菁 译）★★●

4. I was born without a hometown. Home is where my heart settles down.

（王如利 译1）★●●

5. Deep in my heart I've no hometown, where my soul is at ease is where I like to settle down.

（张晓阳 译）●●●

6. For years I have been a stray, and wherever my heart is at ease, I stay.

（冯雷 译） ●●●

7. For a rootless man like me, home is where the heart is.

（王如利 译2） ★●

8. I have had no fixed dwelling place since I was born. But as long as my heart is calm, that place is my hometown.

（董秀静 译） ★★

9. My home is no other than where I can enjoy a peaceful mind.

（石永浩 译1） ●●

10. Since birth I've got no fixed abode; where my heart rests is home.

（马建军 译） ★

11. My home follows my heart.

（石永浩 译2） ★

【130】山不在高，有仙则名；水不在深，有龙则灵。

——刘禹锡《陋室铭》

投票：外方评委6人投票★，中方评委15人投票●

1. Mountains are famous not for their heights but for immortals living there; rivers are not known for their depths but for dragons residing within.

（王绍昌 译） ★★★★★●●●●

2. It is not the height but the residing immortal who makes the mountain well-known; it is not the depth but the dwelling dragon that gives the lake a charming tone.

（冯雷 译1） ★★★●●●●●●●●

3. A mountain excels not by height, with immortals fame it acquires. A lake excels not by depth, with dragons its soul inspires.

(叶如钢 译) ● ● ● ● ● ● ●

4. Mountains stand out not for their height, but for residing immortals; waters shine not for their depth, but for residing dragons.

(乐国斌 译) ★ ★ ★ ● ● ●

5. A mountain needs not to be high; it'd be famed having gods abide. A river needs not to be deep; divine having dragons reside.

(铁冰 译) ★ ● ● ● ● ●

6. The fame of a mountain lies not in its height, but with immortals who might there reside. The nimbus of a river/lake lies not in its depth, but with a dragon hidden beneath.

(王昌玲 译1) ★ ★ ★ ● ●

7. The height of a mountain should make no claim, its immortal residents bring it to fame; the depth of a lake is not always the key, its dwelling dragons create charm and glee.

(冯雷 译2) ★ ● ● ● ●

8. Capital Hill is famous not for its height, but for its heads; red sea is famous not for its depth, but for its redness and salt.

(艾朝阳 译1) ★ ★ ● ●

9. The hill need not be high, immortals lure all to come by. The rill need not be deep, dragons lure all to worship.

(王昌玲 译2) ● ● ● ●

10. It's not height but presence of immortals that really counts for a mountain's fame; it's not depth but residing loongs that really count for waters' name.

(倪庆行 译) ● ● ● ●

名言警句英译

11. A peak, high or low, with immortals will great fame win. A creek, deep or shallow, with loongs will have a sacred mien.

（张俊锋 译1）●●●

12. Mountains win a fame with immortals rather than height; waters get a name by dragons instead of depth.

（曹小菁 译）●●●

13. One is smart not for his hair but for his head; Mona Lisa is live not for her head but for her eyes and smiles.

（艾朝阳 译2）★●

14. Height matters not for a peak: an immortal is its claim to fame. Depth matters not for a creek: a loong will win it a sacred name.

（张俊锋 译2）●●

【131】 曾经沧海难为水，除却巫山不是云。

——元稹《离思五首·其四》

投票：外方评委6人投票★，中方评委6人投票●

1. Those who have seen vast oceans will despise streams; only the clouds girdling Mount Wu coincide with their dreams.

（倪庆行 译）★★★●●●●

2. Once you have been to the pacific, you will find the lakes so small. Once you have climbed to the Everest, you will find no other mountains so tall.

（艾朝阳 译1）★★★●●●●

3. I've seen the greatness of the vast ocean, how could a small pool stir my emotion? I've seen the grandness of the clouds over Mount Wu, how could normal drifting clouds count?

（冯雷 译1）★★●●●

183

4. Just as the sea and Mount Wu have shown the height of beauty, nobody can surpass your beauty in my lovesick eyes.

（乐国斌 译）★ ● ●

5. He will find no other water to attract him because he has the sea of incomparably deep and wide experienced; in addition to the clouds of Mt. Wushan, clouds elsewhere are eclipsed.

（任诚刚 译）★ ●

6. Sea water, once back into river or lake, would feel shame; only those clouds around Mount Wu can claim the name.

（冯雷 译2）★ ●

7. If you once saw the sea, not to visit other rivers you need; except clouds over Mt. Wu, other ones aren't clouds indeed.

（赵宜忠 译）★ ●

8. After I saw bounteous seas, small streams won't me appease; after I encountered gorgeous clouds on Mount Wu, other colored clouds won't me please.

（王绍昌 译）★ ●

9. For love's sake, you are my ocean deep and my mountain high. On all other waters and hills I won't even cast an eye.

（铁冰 译）★ ●

10. I neglect other waters but remember the vast sea of yore; I ignore other clouds as I've seen the mist shrouding the mountain before.

（许霖越 译）● ●

11. After seeing the sea, I admire water elsewhere no more. On appreciating clouds over Wu Mountain, I love other clouds not.

（杨秀波 译）● ●

12. Once in love with you, even Venus can't strike me.

（艾朝阳 译2）★

【132】身无彩凤双飞翼，心有灵犀一点通。

——李商隐《无题·昨夜星辰昨夜风》

投票：外方评委11人投票★，中方评委5人投票●

1. Though our bodies are not paired, yet our soul of love is always shared.

（冯雷 译1）★★★★★★●●●●●

2. We cannot fly in pairs like phoenixes, we do know each other's heart without words.

（董庆瑗 译）★★★★★★★●

3. No phoenix wings to fly, we're apart; we're two harps with one melody at heart.

（叶如钢 译）●●●●●

4. Unlike beautiful phoenix we have no wings to fly side by side; but we have an innate sense to know each other's mind.

（杨中仁 译）★★★★

5. Though we do not own colored wings to fly in pair, yet we do have mutual mind and feelings to share.

（冯雷 译2）●●●●

6. Without the phoenix wings to fly in pair, we do have the magic telepathy to share.

（张俊锋 译）●●●

7. Without wings we cannot fly side by side in the sky; with rapport we can often see eye to eye.

（石永浩 译1）●●●

8. Though our bodies have no phoenix wings soaring high, tacit understanding with meeting of minds can make us fly.

（任诚刚 译）●●

9. We cannot fly together but can think together.

（艾朝阳 译） ★

10. Though we cannot pair off on wings, we often coincide in many things.

（石永浩 译2） ★

【133】不著一字，尽得风流。

——司空图《诗品二十四则·含蓄》

投票：外方评委6人投票★，中方评委2人投票●

1. The art of poetry lies in approaching the subject with subtlety.

（何艳 译） ★ ★ ★ ★ ★

2. The beauty of writing flows between the lines.

（石永浩 译） ★ ★ ★ ●

3. Brevity speaks more eloquently than verbosity.

（叶步青 译） ★ ★ ● ●

4. Literary grace sparkles without a redundant word.

（丁如伟 译） ★ ●

5. Brevity endows readers with endless imagination and appreciation.

（郁序新 译） ★ ●

6. It is the image not the words of a masterpiece that captures its admirers.

（冯雷 译） ★ ●

7. Brief, but graceful.

（曹小菁 译） ★

8. The best writing captures the essence of a fleeting moment with the least words.

（吴春晓 译） ●

9. It is between the lines that poetics lies.

（田璐 译）●

10. Poetry dwells beyond lines; a top-ranking poem elegantly conveys the poet's emotions but uses not a single word to name them.

（铁冰 译）●

11. A splendid writer receives acclaims for using no unnecessary words in writing.

（杨中仁 译）●

【134】不经一番寒彻骨，怎得梅花扑鼻香。

——黄蘖禅师《上堂开示颂》

投票：外方评委10人投票★，中方评委4人投票●

1. Bitter coldness only makes a plum flower more fragrant; hard times only make a man stronger.

（吴春晓 译）★★★★★●●

2. Bitter cold makes plum flowers sweeter; what doesn't kill us makes us stronger.

（铁冰 译）★★★●●●

3. Without weathering a chill piercing into the marrow, plum blossoms would not give out intoxicating fragrance to impinge the nostrils.

（倪庆行 译）★●●

4. No gain, no pain.

（郁序新、关恩亮、王绍昌 译）★●

5. Bitter winter makes wintersweet sweeter.

（王成杰 译）●●

6. Not exposed to the chilling winter, how can wintersweet become fragrant?

（魏红霞 译）●●

7. Without chill all over, how could we appreciate the preciousness of wintersweet blooming in the cold?

（王婷 译）●●

8. Why do plum blossoms smell so sweet? Because they have survived the freezing cold.

（冯雷 译）●●

9. When it snows and the cold is freezing, plum blossoms' scent becomes enchanting.

（叶如钢 译）★

10. The colder it gets, the sweeter the wintersweet is.

（王昌玲 译）★

【135】利在一身勿谋也，利在天下者必谋之。

——钱镠《钱氏家训》

投票：外方评委8人投票★，中方评委4人投票●

1. Seek universal benefits rather than personal ones.

（王昌玲 译）★★★★★●●

2. Seek to benefit the society rather than yourself only.

（石永浩 译）★★●●●

名言警句英译

3. Seek gains for all rather than for your own.

（杨中仁 译）★★●

4. Seek no personal gain, but strive for the good of the country.

（何艳 译）★★●

5. Better altruistic than egoistic.

（刘向军 译）★●

6. Benefits for all always have priority over personal gain.

（冯雷 译）★●

7. Strive for all, not one.

（王成杰 译）★

8. Be sure to seek interests for the people rather than for yourself.

（曹小菁 译）★

【136】问君能有几多愁，恰似一江春水向东流。

——李煜《虞美人·春花秋月何时了》

投票：外方评委6人投票★，中方评委6人投票●

1. If you ask how much I suffer from deprivation and forlornness, take a look, my friend, at the mighty river flowing by.

（石爱伟 译）★★★★★●

2. You ask the tale of my woes; oh, it's long as the river flows.

（张琼 译）★★★★●●

3. Ask myself how much my life is beset with sorrow, as relentlessly as eastward waters ever flow.

（王勋 译）●●●●

4. Do you know how long my grief will last for the loss of my homeland? It's like Yangtze River flowing eastwards with no end.

（张晔 译）●●●●

5. Oh, how is my grief like, do you know? It's like the Yangtze River's ever-running flow!

（铁冰 译）★●●

6. How sad I feel? It flows like the Spring Yangtze River flowing eastward.

（艾朝阳 译1）●●●

7. Being asked, my sorrow, to what is it comparable? Like the river, filled by spring, flowing, inexhaustible.

（李开林 译）★★

8. My sorrow weighs as much as the spring water in the Yangtze River, and lasts as long as the River runs eastwards.

（艾朝阳 译2）★●

9. How sorrow do I have if ye ask? Just like endless water flowing in an eastward river.

（乐国斌 译）●●

10. You may ask how much grief I feel in my heart, as if spring tides run to east to tear me apart.

（郁序新 译）●●

11. If you ask how much sorrow I feel, it's like the spring river flowing east.

（魏红霞 译）★

12. Shall I ask how sorrowful you are? The endless vernal river flowing eastward will be a perfect metaphor.

（倪庆行 译）★

名言警句英译

【137】近水楼台先得月，向阳花木易为春。——苏麟《断句》

投票：外方评委6人投票★，中方评委8人投票●

1. Waterfront buildings first enjoy the moon's beautiful reflection, sun-facing plants easily receive the spring's warm affection.

（冯雷 译1）★★★★★●●●

2. Waterside buildings are first to share moonlight, sun-facing flowers are first to share spring might.

（程永生 译）●●●●●

3. Terraces bordering water gets first moonbeams; flowers facing sun enjoy early blooms.

（王绍昌 译）●●●●

4. Waterside towers get moon's reflection; sunward flowers have spring's affection.

（叶如钢 译）★●●

5. Waterfront towers savor the moonlight first, sunward flowers are favored to make the spring burst.

（刘群 译）★●●

6. The water-adjoining tower overlooks the moon first; the sun-bathed plants receive the sunshine best.

（石永浩 译）●●●

7. When moon rises, the towers near water get the best view; when spring arrives, the plants facing the sun are among the first to renew.

（冯雷 译2）●●●

8. The towers near the water can get the moon projection firstly; and the flowers and trees facing the sun germinate early.

（赵宜忠 译）●●

9. Waterside pavilions are first to enjoy the moonlight; sun-facing plants are first to make a spring.

（乐国斌 译）● ●

10. The pavilion adjacent to waters will be the first to enjoy the moon; trees and flowers facing the sun will thrive soon.

（倪庆行 译）● ●

11. Reflected first with the moon are waterside buildings, bloom easily those sunlit flowers into spring.

（杨秀波 译）● ●

12. Platform near water baths the moon beam first; flowers and trees facing the sun approach spring in way easy and fast.

（任诚刚 译）● ●

13. It's easier for people on the waterside to appreciate the Moon, and faster for plants facing the Sun to shoot.

（曹小菁 译）★

【138】诗是无形画，画是有形诗。——张舜民《跋百之诗画》

投票：外方评委6人投票★，中方评委5人投票●

1. Poetry paints without picture, while paintings poetize with color.

（张俊锋 译）★ ★ ★ ★ ●

2. Poetry is drawing in words, and drawing is poetry in lines.

（曹小菁 译1）★ ★ ● ●

3. Poetry is painting and painting is poetry, though one is composed with letters but the other is created by colors.

（曹小菁 译2）● ● ●

4. Poetry can be picturesque as painting. Painting can be poetic as poetry.

（王昌玲 译）★ ●

5. Poetry is intangible painting, and painting tangible poetry.

（石永浩 译）★ ★

6. Poetry is invisible painting, and painting is visible poetry.

（任诚刚 译1）● ●

7. Painting draws with poetic line; poem paints with picture fine. You see it means you have imagination here; you don't see it but it still hides there.

（任诚刚 译2）● ●

8. Poetry is an invisible painting only, but a painting is the visible poetry.

（赵宜忠 译）★

9. Poems depict what one sees in words, while paintings express what one thinks in colors.

（魏红霞 译）★

【139】不立异以为高，不逆情以干誉。——欧阳修《纵囚论》

投票：外方评委5人投票★，中方评委2人投票●

1. Do not take unconventional behavior as noble; do not do unreasonable things to seek fame.

（任诚刚 译）★ ★ ★ ●

2. Do not make yourself conspicuous by acting differently or going against common sense on purpose.

（董秀静 译）★ ●

3. Don't take novelty for distinction, nor seek fame at the cost of humanity.

(王如利 译) ★★

4. Never stand out with novelty and never seek reputation with perversity.

(倪庆行 译) ●●

5. Show not nobility by being different; seek not fame by being perverse.

(王成杰 译) ●●

6. Never seek nobility by doing something against convention or fish for fame by acting against human nature.

(王毅 译) ★

7. Neither pretend to be wise by being different, nor seek fame via betraying good conscience.

(吴春晓 译) ★

8. Don't be unconventional to look noble, nor sacrifice your principles for fame.

(马建军 译) ●

9. Neither seek to be different as superior, nor violate reason to earn one's reputation.

(杨秀波 译) ●

【140】 出淤泥而不染，濯清涟而不妖。——周敦颐《爱莲说》

投票：外方评委9人投票★，中方评委6人投票●

1. Rooted in pond sludge, the lotus remains pure; bathed in rippling water, the lotus stays demure.

(石永浩 译1) ★★★★●●●●●

2. Born out of dirty mud, the lotus stays free of dirt; rising above rippling water, it sways but does not flirt.

(石永浩 译2) ●●●●●

3. Unstained while growing out of dark mud, unspoiled after bathing in a clear pond.

(樊功生 译) ★●●●

4. Emerging from slimy mud, the lotus remains fresh and pure; standing atop rippling water, the lotus maintains graceful attire.

(王绍昌 译) ●●●●

5. Lotus grows in mud but keeps pure, and dances amid ripples but looks demure.

(曹小菁 译) ★●●

6. I am partial to the lotus because of its purity though it grows out of black mud and its lack of affectation though it is adorned with crystal water beads.

(石爱伟 译) ★★★

7. Out of the mire, yet the lotus remains undefiled. Washed by clear water, it looks charming rather than flirting.

(彭智鹏 译) ●●●

8. Growing out of mire, lotus is spotlessly pure; bathing in ripples, it is pretty but not flirty.

(王昌玲 译1) ●●

9. Rising up from mud, lotus is spotless. Out from tender water, it has the grace of a goddess.

(叶如钢 译) ●●

10. The thick silt where it grows brings no dirty stain to its nature; the rippling water where it bathes adds no seductive charm to its look.

(冯雷 译) ★

11. Being pure and lofty in nature, lotus is never influenced by ooze and water.

（杨秀波 译）★

12. Grown from mud, lotus keeps itself free from mud; and after bathed in clear water, it becomes as chaste as the water.

（段冰知 译）★

13. Grown out of mud, the lotus appears not muddied; graced by clear ripples, she is fair but not coquettish.

（铁冰 译）★

14. Unaffected by the environment, dirty or flirty, the lotus remains pure and plain.

（王昌玲 译2）★

15. Born out of slimy mud, the lotus is pure and stainless; bathed in clear ripples, she is charming yet not coquettish.

（张俊锋 译）★

【141】穷视其所不为，贫视其所不取。

——司马光《资治通鉴·周纪一》

投票：外方评委4人投票★，中方评委3人投票●

1. One's decision in adversity reveals his true beliefs.

（冯雷 译）★★●

2. A man's virtues can be seen from what he doesn't do in times of adversity or what he doesn't take when in poverty.

（叶如钢 译）●●●

3. You can judge a person's moral quality by observing what he refuses to do when frustrated and what he refuses to grasp when being poor.

（董秀静 译）★ ●

4. To judge a person, we must see what he refuses to do in desperation and what he does not take in dire needs.

（石爱伟 译）● ●

5. The best way to know a person is to see what he would do when in poverty or under disadvantageous circumstances.

（王梅兰 译）★

6. A man's character is revealed by his deeds and attitudes in poverty or adversity.

（王毅 译）★

7. Judge a man by what he refuses when penniless and frustrated.

（王成杰 译）★

8. It is advisable to judge a man by what he refrains from in times of difficulty.

（刘雪芹 译）●

9. To judge a man, you must inspect what he does and what he pursues when he's poor.

（杨中仁 译）●

10. To judge a person's moral integrity, see whether he takes ill-gotten gains when he's poor and underachieving.

（董庆瑗 译）●

【142】为天地立心，为生民立命，为往圣继绝学，为万世开太平。

——张载《横渠四句》

投票：外方评委4人投票★，中方评委2人投票●

1. The four missions of intellectuals: establishing conscience between heaven and earth; facilitating happy life for human beings; securing renaissance of the lost teachings of ancient sages; and creating everlasting peace for the whole world.

（铁冰 译）★★★★●●

2. Explore the way of nature and human mind for their unification; enlighten the common people on fulfilling the vocation; carry on suspended Confucianism of the ancient sages; create a peaceful world that will go through all ages.

（张俊锋 译）★●●

3. Our sacred missions are to spread benevolence and fraternity all over the world, to improve the people's living conditions, to inherit the past sages' doctrines and to forge eternal peace.

（倪庆行 译）★●

4. Here is my dream—to seek the truth of the universe, to guide the people for a better life, to retain the wisdom of past sages, to forward the striving for human peace, always, and forever.

（李开林 译）★

5. (A SAINT AIMS) to understand and follow the law of nature, to improve the spiritual value of the people, to complete the academic system of the former holy inheritance, and to establish the foundation of peace and order for the world of later generations.

（冯雷 译）●

名言警句英译

6. The sage is determined to explore the nature, serve the people, inherit the past sages, and create peace for future generations.

（艾朝阳 译）●

【143】腹有诗书气自华。——苏轼《和董传留别》

投票：外方评委12人投票★，中方评委14人投票●

1. Culture inside, elegance outside.

（曹小菁 译1）★★★★★●●●●●●●

2. Reading makes one cultivated.

（曹小菁 译2）★★★★★★★●●

3. To be learned is to be tempered.

（彭智鹏 译）★★★★★★★●

4. He who is well read radiates elegance.

（刘群 译1）★★★★★★★●

5. The poetry and literature inside, the confidence and temperament outside.

（姜玉玮 译）★★●●●●●●

6. Books are the best cosmetics.

（李红雨 译）★★●●●●

7. Book fragrance nurtures your elegance.

（石永浩 译）●●●●●●

8. Profound knowledge makes the man.

（王勐 译）★★★●●

9. A well-read man cannot hide his elegance.

（冯雷 译1）★★●●●

10. Readings make the man and the manners.

（王绍昌 译1）★●●●

11. Poetry and the book, add charm to one's look.

（冯雷 译2）★★★

12. Steeping yourself in poetry books will enhance elegance on your looks.

（倪庆行 译1）●●●

13. Graces within, elegances without.

（王绍昌 译2）●●●

14. Knowledge cultivates an elegant character.

（张顺生 译）★★

15. Reading cultivates elegant demeanor.

（刘群 译2）●●

16. He who's steeped in poetry oozes charm.

（王昌玲 译）★

17. Books enhance looks.

（倪庆行 译2）★

18. He who reads fragrant books often smells fragrant.

（艾朝阳 译）★

【144】人有悲欢离合，月有阴晴圆缺，此事古难全。

——苏轼《水调歌头·明月几时有》

投票：外方评委5人投票★，中方评委3人投票●

1. Man has joys and woes at life's beckon; the moon waxes and wanes in turn. 'Tis the universal law that's in reign.

（王昌玲 译）★★★●

2. Life is always parting or meeting, and sorrow or delight, as Moon may be partial or full, and dim or bright.

（叶如钢 译）★ ★ ★ ●

3. Joy and sorrow, union and departure, such is life; wax and wane, such is the moon. It's always hard to fulfill as you wish.

（彭智鹏 译）★ ★ ●

4. Men may meet or part, having joy or pain, as the moon bright or dim, may wax or wane: since of yore nothing can perfect remain.

（铁冰 译）★ ● ●

5. Like the moon waxing or waning, we part tearful or meet joyful. Never have things all occurred as we wish.

（石永浩 译）★ ●

6. Meeting or parting, joy or sorrow, people answer fate's call; waxing or waning, shiny or shady, the moon can't control.

（乐国斌 译）● ●

7. Since ancient times, it has always been regrettable but unchangeable that happy or sad, human beings gather and part, and bright or dim, the moon waxes and wanes.

（曹小菁 译）● ●

8. The moon waxes and wanes, your dear comes and goes; the moon turns full and narrow, our life is happiness and sorrow; for both human and nature, imperfection is universal.

（冯雷 译）★

9. Humans meet and depart, the moon waxes and wanes. It's the imperfect law of life and nature since of old.

（王绍昌 译）★

【145】但愿人长久，千里共婵娟。

——苏轼《水调歌头·明月几时有》

投票：外方评委 5 人投票★，中方评委 4 人投票●

1. Wish my honey well forever, then even far away from each other, we'll appreciate the moon together.

（曹小菁 译） ★●●●●

2. We are one thousand miles apart, the moon looks always dear to our heart; may we live in peace and long, enjoying the world where we belong.

（冯雷 译） ★★●●

3. Wish the ones you love live long without care; even if far apart, the moon you can share.

（魏红霞 译） ★★●

4. May we be well for ever, and share the bright, full moon of reunion so fair, every mid-autumn night, even though far apart.

（张俊锋 译） ★★★

5. May we all be blessed with longevity. Though thousands of miles apart, we can still share the beautiful moonlight together.

（赵宜忠 译） ★★★

6. May we all enjoy a long happy life; may the graceful moon witness our life of love.

（乐国斌 译 1） ★★

7. Far apart, we are stars scattered on the ground; nothing sad, for all are blessed to live safe and sound, to share the generous light that the moon has shed.

（李开林 译） ★★

8. I'd wish all families stay long around; even far apart, bask in the same moon round.

（王昌玲 译）●●

9. Wish we can live long, and enjoy the bright moon together no matter we are thousand-mile away.

（任诚刚 译）★

10. May the moon watch over us all to live a long and joyful life.

（乐国斌 译2）★

11. Long live you and me though now far apart, but we can share the moon who'll not depart.

（程永生 译）★

【146】旧书不厌百回读，熟读深思子自知。

——苏轼《送安惇秀才失解西归》

投票：外方评委9人投票★，中方评委6人投票●

1. Classics are worth reading again and again. Reflection renders their deepest meaning plain.

（王昌玲 译）★★★★★★★●●●

2. Intensive reading and deep thinking give you insight into the truths in the classics.

（王成杰 译）★★★●●●

3. Classics are to be read many times, for the more you read, the more you meditate, and the more you acquire.

（马建军 译）★●●

4. Classics are worth reading a hundred times, whose essence can be captured by repeated chewing and digesting.

（王毅 译）● ● ●

5. Delving into classics time and again, fresh insights you always gain.

（石永浩 译）● ● ●

6. Old books should be read again and again, think deeply to grasp the treasures they contain.

（叶如钢 译）★ ●

7. Read good books keenly to reap your insight deeply.

（崔传明 译）★ ●

8. Old books are worth myriad reading. Perceptions are gained via repeated perusing and pondering.

（王绍昌 译）● ●

9. A good old book is worth reading many times, and each time we understand better.

（吴春晓 译）★

10. Read over the old book and you'll grasp its old roots.

（王梅兰 译）★

11. It is always inviting to read the classics. Deep thought with constant reading familiarizes you with it.

（杨秀波 译）★

12. Books need to be repeatedly read and thought about.

（陶家乐 译）★

13. One should not be tired of rereading an old book because each reading leads to contemplation and a better understanding.

（孙玲玲 译）★

14. A clever reader becomes wise by reading classic books multiple times.

（冯雷 译）★

【147】恃大而不戒，则轻敌而屡败；知小而自畏，则深谋而必克。

——苏轼《策断二十四》

投票：外方评委8人投票★，中方评委4人投票●

1. Pride and taking the rivals lightly make the strong fall; courage and planning carefully make the weak rise.

（王成杰 译）★★★★★●●

2. The strong man is often defeated for underestimating his rival, whereas the weak beats his rival for forethought.

（杨中仁 译）★★★★

3. A strong army may belittle the enemy and ends up defeated; a weak army may be vigilant and prudent and thus wins victory.

（王昌玲 译）★●●

4. A strong state, if off-guard, is doomed to failures for taking its enemy lightly. A weak state, if circumspect, can vanquish its enemy by laying careful plans.

（王毅 译）●●●

5. Slighting the enemy with an overconfident mindset incurs defeat; proper evaluation of one's own strength in a discreet manner ensures victory.

（石爱伟 译）★●

6. Fearlessness issued from arrogance results in losses; deliberations bred from humbleness lead to victories.

（王绍昌 译）★★

7. Underestimation undermines.

（杨胜悦 译）●●

8. Staying alert matters. Countries big but not alert may belittle their enemies and lose battles, while countries small but alert may gain the victory
through considerable planning.

（马建军 译）● ●

9. The strong often fail because they hardly guard against their arrogance
and recklessness; the weak often win because they feel awe and are always
well-prepared.

（冯雷 译）★

【148】山无陵，天地合，乃敢与君绝。

——语本《乐府诗集·鼓吹曲辞·上邪》

投票：外方评委8人投票★，中方评委8人投票●

1. Until crumble the mountains high, and the earth mingle with the sky, will
my love for you die.

（铁冰 译）★ ★ ● ● ● ● ● ● ●

2. My love, I promise to remain true to you until mountains melt away, and
there's no night or day!

（冯雷 译）★ ★ ★ ★ ★ ● ● ●

3. Even the mountain turns into a plain, or heaven and earth mingle together again, my love for you shall forever remain.

（王毅 译）★ ★ ● ● ● ● ●

4. My love to you will last long till mountains are flat and heaven and earth
combine in one.

（杨中仁 译）★ ★ ★ ★ ●

5. If no hills can be seen, and the sky becomes the sea; then I'd stop loving thee.

（魏红霞 译）★★★●●

6. Never shall I part from thee unless mountains lost their ridges or heaven and earth merged.

（刘群 译）★★★●

7. Mountains may be flattened, heavens may fall on the land. My love for you knows no end.

（石爱伟 译1）★●●

8. When mountains had no top, should heaven to earth drop. My love for thee would stop.

（王昌玲 译1）★●●

9. Thou art the eternal love in my heart, even the mighty of heaven and earth mingled together cannot tear our love apart.

（郁序新 译1）★●●

10. Our love stands there even if the mountain flattened, sky-earth no distance.

（魏东海 译）★●

11. Nothing can betray my vow of love to you, unless mountains fall to flat, heaven and Earth melt into one.

（郁序新 译2）★●

12. I dare betray you, my love. Only when mountains topple, heaven and earth mingle.

（石爱伟 译2）★●

13. Unless mountains were flattened to the ground and the sky fell to the earth, I could part from thee.

（赵宜忠 译）★●

14. Should mountains fall or heaven collapses, till these do us part.

（彭智鹏 译）●●

15. How long is my love for thee? As long as mountains stand, as long as sky's above land.

（王昌玲 译2）●●

16. Only dare I cease my love for you when mountains disappear and the hell and heaven mix together.

（李东超 译）★

17. Our love and devotion will survive the crumbling of mountains and fall of sky.

（樊功生 译）★

【149】鲜衣怒马少年时，不负韶华行且知。

——语本岳飞《鹊桥仙》："鲜衣怒马少年时。"

投票：外方评委7人投票★，中方评委3人投票●

1. Youth, glorious and beautiful. Let's live it to the fullest with passion.

（马建军 译）★★★★

2. Precious is the vigorous youth. Let's honor its glory by learning and doing.

（田璐 译）★●●

3. Young gallants, armour yourselves, mount your steeds, seize the time to realize your dreams.

（王昌玲 译）●●●

名言警句英译

4. Youth is the time of bright colour and high spirit, live up to it by practicing and learning.

（何艳 译）★ ●

5. Riding gallant horses and in shining dresses, the prodigies are on the way to accomplish the missions of their times.

（叶如钢 译 1）● ●

6. Galloping on my steed, I am in the prime. Cherishing lofty ideals, I am biding my time.

（石永浩 译）● ●

7. Be ambitious and plan for your future when you are vigorously young.

（王梅兰 译）★

8. Beautifully, Eileen Gu achieves one splendid goal after another, living up to the highest expectations.

（叶如钢 译 2）★

9. Fine garment he wears and fine horse he rides, a young man. Must remember he use the prime of life to achieve what he can.

（石爱伟 译）★

10. Do cherish your young days to pursue your dream.

（张晓阳 译）★

11. With the beautiful and energetic youth blooming, let's live up to it by learning and doing.

（王如利 译）★

12. Keep true to the dreams of your youth.

（郁序新 译, 借用 Friedrich Schiller）★

【150】 山重水复疑无路，柳暗花明又一村。

——陆游《游山西村》

投票：外方评委9人投票★，中方评委6人投票●

1. Ahead, the mountain obstructing, the river winding, it seems the road has come to an end. However, all of a sudden, a village arises in green willows and bright flowers.

（李红雨 译）★★★★★★★●

2. Many a time mountains and rivers made me think the road would be a dead end, yet green willows and fresh flowers welcomed me to another village, and my path would extend.

（冯雷 译）★★★★●●●

3. Amid stretching hills and winding rills, I fear no path can be found; through dense willow trees and bright flowers, I spot another village around.

（许霖越 译）★●●●●●

4. I seem to have come to the world's end with mountains and rivers, yet a hamlet springs up with green willows and bright flowers.

（张俊锋 译）★★★●

5. There seems no road but hills and rills in my sight, but another village looms within willows green and blooms bright.

（赵宜忠 译1）●●●●

6. Am I lost along a meandering brook amid hills? After willows and flaming flowers a hamlet reveals!

（王昌玲 译）★★★

7. Amidst ridges and rivers there seems no trail through; among willows and flowers a hamlet jumps into view.

（石永浩 译）★●●

8. Hill after hill and rill after rill everywhere, but no way in doubt; suddenly appears another village with willows and blooms about.

（赵宜忠 译2） ●●

9. No way to go it seems, new hope to see it comes.

（任诚刚 译） ★

10. Wrapped in hills and rivers, the road ahead seems lost; enclosed amid dim willows and bright blooms, another village doth loom.

（王绍昌 译） ★

【151】古人学问无遗力，少壮工夫老始成。
——陆游《冬夜读书示子聿》

投票：外方评委5人投票★，中方评委4人投票●

1. The ancients spared no effort for knowledge; the pains taken in youth paid off in old age.

（石永浩 译1） ★★●●●●

2. Ancient scholars all took great pains to learn. Youth's efforts bring profound learning in return.

（王昌玲 译） ★★●●

3. In the old books I see tears and sweats, then I learn that the efforts in youth are justified in age.

（艾朝阳 译） ★★★

4. To learning ancient scholars gave their all, striving since youth and fruiting in life's fall.

（叶如钢 译） ●●●

5. Young, to learn, ancients strain every nerve; old, the accomplishment they deserve.

（魏红霞 译）★ ●

6. In learning ancients take all steps, hard and bold; germination, young; fruition, old.

（王绍昌 译）● ●

7. Ancient scholars spared no pains in learning, achieving greatly only through decades' striving.

（石永浩 译2）● ●

8. The ancients tried their best to learn all out. Studying hard in youth they gained in old age no doubt.

（赵宜忠 译）● ●

9. To acquire knowledge the ancients labor, thus fruits are only reaped with early endeavor.

（刘群 译）★

【152】天下之事，常成于困约，而败于奢靡。

——陆游《放翁家训》

投票：外方评委8人投票★，中方评委4人投票●

1. Great results are often achieved by those struggling in hardship; things are ruined time and again due to extravagance.

（叶如钢 译，投票后修改）★ ★ ★ ★ ★ ★

2. Difficulties and restraints may often propel one to success whereas comforts and excesses will land one in failure.

（叶步青 译）★ ★ ★ ●

3. While hardships breed success, achievements fall apart in extravagance.

（田璐 译）★★●●

4. More often than not, while success comes from hardship, failure stems from extravagance.

（何艳 译）★★●●

5. When in poverty, people will strive for success. When in abundance, people lose their ambition.

（董庆瑗 译）★★★

6. Success sprouts from striving; extravagance breeds failure.

（王成杰 译）★★●

7. Rise in distress, and you will succeed; wallow in extravagance, and you will fail. This is a universal truth.

（倪庆行 译）●●●

8. Prosperity buds in adversity; decadence brews in extravagance.

（石永浩 译）●●●

9. Discipline and regulation lead to success; indulgence and luxury result in failure.

（王梅兰 译）★●

10. Poverty motivates one to strive for success, while luxury leads him to failure.

（王昌玲 译）★●

11. Hardships bring up accomplishment; extravagance leads to failure.

（冯雷 译）★●

12. Simplicity and difficulty make one succeed, while luxury and prodigality make one fail.

（魏红霞 译）●●

13. Everything in the world follows the pattern that thrifty and economy bring achievement and extravagance and wastage incur failure.

（丁如伟 译）●●

14. Like anything in the world, success thrives on adversities, and failure follows wastefulness.

（樊功生 译）★

【153】文章本天成，妙手偶得之。——陆游《文章》

投票：外方评委8人投票★，中方评委5人投票●

1. Great articles seem nature-endowed, casually penned by a master hand.

（王昌玲 译）★●●●●●

2. Good writing comes where serendipity plays a part.

（吴春晓 译）★★★★★★

3. Beautiful poems come about naturally, even a gifted poet only writes one once in a while.

（叶如钢 译）★★★★

4. A well-written essay is a natural piece of art, writing it takes the author's subtle mind and heart.

（石爱伟 译）●●●●

5. Knowledge and spontaneous creativity allow for great writing.

（陶家乐 译）★★★

6. Essays are natural in essence; skilled writers capture them by sheer coincidence.

（丁如伟 译）★●

7. Essays are perfected by natural experiences. Talents compile them by chance.

（张立国 译）★★

8. Poetry is an art of heaven, and clever men get it only by chance.

（樊功生 译）★★

9. A good article is like nature itself discovered incidentally by a skilled writer.

（田璐 译）★★

10. The fine pieces of writing are often composed by the talented writers with proficient writing skills and inspirations.

（杨中仁 译）●●

11. A masterpiece is a natural creation occasionally made by a master.

（王梅兰 译）●●

12. The good article originates in the expression of natural way through the inspiration of a writer by chance.

（郁序新 译）★

13. Excellent articles are generally made by nature and gained occasionally through inspiration and ingenious technique.

（史红霞 译）★

【154】位卑未敢忘忧国，事定犹须待阖棺。

——陆游《病起书怀》

投票：外方评委 3 人投票★，中方评委 2 人投票●

1. Though humble, I never forget my responsibilities for the country, and only after death will I be finally judged.

（王成杰 译）★★●

2. Care about your nation whoever you are, make no verdict before things are clear.

（刘德江 译）★

3. I never forget concerning the state affairs though I'm in a low position, my loyalty to the country will be fairly witnessed after my decease.

（郁序新 译）●

4. Humble as I am, I'll still concern myself with state affairs. Not until after one's death will he earn his reputation final and fair.

（王毅 译）●

5. Lower status won't stop me from serving my country heart and soul; only an after-death evaluation will show my merits as a whole.

（冯雷 译）●

6. Humble as I am, I'll be deeply concerned about the fate of the nation, for the judgement is only made after the coffin lid is closed.

（马建军 译）●

7. Humble as I am, worries about our nation never leave my heart; reunification of the land cannot be seen until this life I depart.

（石永浩 译）●

【155】 海阔凭鱼跃，天高任鸟飞。

——语本阮阅《诗话总龟前集》：“大海从鱼跃，长空任鸟飞。”

投票：外方评委9人投票★，中方评委6人投票●

1. In the boundless oceans, fish can swim far and wide; in the limitless heavens, birds can soar or glide.

（石永浩 译）★★★★★★★★●●●●

名言警句英译

2. The sea is broad enough for fish to dive; the sky is vast enough for birds to soar.

(冯雷 译) ★★★★★★★●

3. Generous is the ocean for ambitious fish; lofty is the sky for aspiring birds.

(铁冰 译1) ★★★★

4. In the broad ocean leap and dive freely can the fish; on the infinite sky can the birds fly as high as they wish.

(任诚刚 译) ●●●

5. A vast ocean allows fish to swim their fill; a high sky embraces birds of lofty will.

(铁冰 译2) ●●●

6. The sky is a boundless stage for birds, so is the ocean for fish.

(李开林 译) ★●

7. So vast is the sea for fish to leap; so high is the sky for birds to fly.

(彭智鹏 译) ★●

8. Fish delve deep and wide; birds fly high and far. The world's the best playground for all talented people, whoever you are.

(王绍昌 译) ★★

9. The vast sea is for giant fish to swim. The deep sky is for mighty birds to soar.

(王昌玲 译) ●●

10. Endless sea endues sharks with fin to dive freely; boundless sky endows birds with wings to fly lightly.

(郁序新 译) ●●

【156】以责人之心责己，以恕己之心恕人。

——范公偁《过庭录》

投票：外方评委7人投票★，中方评委2人投票●

1. Be as strict with yourself as you are with others；be as lenient with others as you are with yourself.

（王成杰 译）★★★★●

2. Be critical of yourself as you are of others；be tolerant of others as you are of yourself.

（王慧玉 译）★★★★●

3. Blame yourself as you blame others, and forgive others as you forgive yourself.

（张晓阳 译）★★●

4. Blame yourself the way you blame others；forgive others the way you forgive yourself.

（何艳、田璐 译）★●●

5. Criticize yourself as strongly as you criticize others. Forgive others as easily as you forgive yourself.

（何冰 译）★★★

6. We should blame ourselves the way we blame others and forgive others the way we forgive ourselves.

（董秀静 译）★★★

7. Criticize yourself as you do others，forgive others as you do yourself.

（叶如钢 译）★●

8. Judge yourself at least as harshly as you judge others. Forgive others at least as easily as you forgive yourself.

（马建军 译）★★

9. Be strict with yourself and be generous with others.

（郁序新 译） ★

10. Blame others the way you blame yourself. Forgive others the way you forgive yourself.

（王梅兰 译） ★

11. Blame yourself as you would blame others；forgive others as you would forgive yourself.

（冯雷 译） ★

【157】工贵其久，业贵其专。——陈亮《耘斋铭》

投票：外方评委6人投票★，中方评委5人投票●

1. Perseverance and focus determine everything.

（陈金金 译） ★ ★ ★ ★ ★

2. Perseverance and devotion are essential in making achievements.

（王成杰 译） ★ ★ ● ●

3. Devotion and perseverance are critical to success.

（王毅 译） ★ ★ ● ●

4. The most important elements in doing something are perseverance and concentration.

（杨秀波 译） ★ ★ ●

5. The key to make success lies in perseverance and concentration.

（郁序新 译） ● ● ●

6. It takes time and focus to perfect workmanship.

（王绍昌 译） ★ ●

7. For a craft, what really counts is enduring. For a career, what really counts is professional.

（倪庆行 译）●●

8. The quality of the craftwork lies in the time you spend; the value of the profession comes from the depth you learn.

（孙玲玲 译）●●

9. To master a skill requires persistence, to carve out a career demands dedication.

（何艳 译）●●

10. Priority should be given to persistence and concentration.

（魏红霞 译）★

【158】问世间情为何物，直教人生死相许。

——元好问《摸鱼儿·雁丘词》

投票：外方评委7人投票★，中方评委4人投票●

1. What makes love so nice that it is even worth life being the price?

（石永浩 译）★●●●●

2. What is love I know not; without love I live not.

（乐国斌 译）★★●●

3. I love you without knowing how and why, if you leave me I'd rather choose to die.

（冯雷 译, 前半句部分借用 Neruda 爱情诗）★●●

4. What's love on earth that lovers give each other all even life and death?

（彭智鹏 译）★●●

5. What on earth is in love that compels people to pledge with their lives!

（刘群 译）★★★

6. May I ask everyone in the world what love is after all, and why lovers can give up their lives for it over all.

（赵宜忠 译）★●

7. What is love on earth? For it even life one is willing to sacrifice.

（曹小菁 译1）★●

8. What, may we ask, is love on earth, to which one devotes life and death?

（叶如钢 译1）★★

9. What is Love? Who in this world could ever tell? For it men live, and would vow to die!

（铁冰 译）★★

10. What on earth is love, I sigh, for which people live and die.

（叶如钢 译2）●●

11. None knows what love really is, for which all could be quit.

（曹小菁 译2）★

【159】春色满园关不住，一枝红杏出墙来。

——叶绍翁《游园不值》

投票：外方评委9人投票★，中方评委8人投票●

1. O'er the wall a spray of red-apricot does sway; a gardenful of spring charm is given away.

（石永浩 译）★★★★★●●●●

2. How could the vigor and vitality of spring be possibly locked away? Over the garden wall, I see a twig of red-apricot stretch out and sway!

（冯雷 译）● ● ● ● ● ●

3. A garden can't hold the splendor of spring inside, where a twig of red apricot stretches out.

（杨中仁 译）★ ★ ★ ★ ★

4. A country garden is full of springtime blooming, and a stem of apricots dangles out blushing.

（樊功生 译）● ● ● ● ●

5. A profusion of spring scenes cannot be contained in the garden at all, with a spray of scarlet apricot blossom protruding beyond the wall.

（倪庆行 译）● ● ● ●

6. The spring scenery cannot be shut in the garden at all, because a branch of red apricots comes out of the wall.

（赵宜忠 译）● ● ●

7. The garden can't imprison the spring at all: on a twig of red apricot she stretches out the wall.

（铁冰 译）● ● ●

8. Spring scenes in the garden can't be locked out; out of wall, a branch of apricots tout.

（魏红霞 译）★ ●

9. The garden can't stand being filled with spring beauty any more, a spray of red apricot heads out of the wall.

（张晓阳 译）● ●

10. Fence can't have the spring flowers or trees enveloped, among which apricot outstretches one twig, brightly red!

（李开林 译）● ●

11. The permeated spring can't be closed within the garden. Out of its wall a red apricot branch full of blossoms reaches out.

（杨秀波 译）●●

12. Blossom fairies overflow in the court, nothing can cage them at all; a pink arm like apricot stretches out, flirting with passers on the wall.

（郁序新 译）★

【160】人生自古谁无死，留取丹心照汗青。

——文天祥《过零丁洋》

投票：外方评委 10 人投票★，中方评委 3 人投票●

1. We all die, but patriots are remembered.

（王成杰 译）★★★★★★★★★★●

2. Humans all eventually die, but a death without meaning is worthless.

（陶家乐 译）★★●

3. No man is immortal, but a loyal heart stays forever.

（陈金金 译）★★●

4. One's life is mortal, but his heartful devotion to his country is immortal.

（艾朝阳 译）★●

5. None have escaped death since the ancient times. I would leave my loyal heart illuminating in history.

（王薇 译）★

6. Better to die for a place in the National Heroes Hall of Fame, than to live as a slave leaving behind a bad name.

（刘向军 译）★

7. Who has ever escaped from death since antiquity? I'll leave my loyalty to shine in the pages of history.

(张晓阳 译) ●

8. Nobody can avert death in this world, I will put my loyalty to the state.

(郁序新 译) ●

9. Of all human beings from Death who can be? Patriotism immortalizes me!

(王昌玲 译) ●

10. Since olden days no man but dies; in the annals my name ever shines!

(吴伟雄 译) ●

11. From days of yore till now who dies never? Leave noble glory to shine forever.

(叶如钢 译) ●

12. Although death comes to all men with no exception; let history annals be illuminated with my loyalty and dedication.

(冯雷 译) ●

13. Can anyone not die since ancient times? In history, only a loyal heart shines.

(魏红霞 译) ●

14. Death befalls all men alike. Only the stout-hearted leave their shining examples behind.

(叶步青 译) ●

15. One is born only for death in the end. Why not die for a good and patriotic cause?

(孙玲玲 译) ●

16. A man is doomed to die since ancient times, yet a patriotic heart shines bright in history.

(何艳 译) ●

17. All men will die someday, but dying for my motherland will see my loyalty shine through the annals of history.

（石永浩 译）●

【161】酒逢知己千杯少，话不投机半句多。

——《名贤集·七言集》

投票：外方评委9人投票★，中方评委6人投票●

1. With a soul mate, drinking a thousand cups of wine is far from enough. With an uncongenial person, uttering half a word is too much.

（倪庆行 译）★★★★●●●●

2. A thousand cups of wine is no big deal, when drinking with a soulmate; in the presence of a repugnant man one word is too many.

（石爱伟 译）★★★★●●

3. A thousand cups of wines are too few when one drinks with a bosom friend, while half a sentence is too much when one disputes with another.

（郁序新 译）★★●●●●

4. When drinking with your bosom friend, a thousand cups would not be the end; when speaking to someone with nothing to share, even one more word you would not bear.

（冯雷 译1）★●●●●

5. Exchanges between soulmates can last over one thousand glasses of wine; to communicate with a difficult person, it is unnecessary to produce even half a line.

（冯雷 译2）●●●●●

6. Drinking with an alter ego can happily go on and on, while even one word is too much when a conversation goes wrong.

（叶如钢 译）★ ★ ● ●

7. With a bosom friend together, you may talk and drink no end, while with a disagreeable guy, you must feel a word is more than need.

（杨中仁 译）★ ★ ★ ★

8. When facing a bosom friend, even a thousand glasses of wine seems not enough; facing a disagreeable person, even exchanging one word seems to be too many.

（杨秀波 译）● ● ● ●

9. For friends to stay in glee, congeniality is the key.

（王绍昌 译）★ ●

10. Even a ton of wine is too little for cheerful congenial friends; even a single word is too much for a disagreeable chat.

（铁冰 译）★

11. For congenial ones, even a thousand cups of liquor is not enough to drink together; while for uncongenial ones, even half a sentence is too many to talk.

（段冰知 译）★

【162】路遥知马力，日久见人心。——陈元靓《事林广记》

投票：外方评委8人投票★，中方评委6人投票●

1. Distance tests a horse's potential. Time shows the nature of a heart.

（杨秀波 译）★ ★ ★ ● ●

2. For a horse's stamina, distance tells; for a person's heart, time reveals.

(倪庆行 译) ★●●●●

3. As a long trip trials a gallant horse, a long time reveals a true heart.

(彭智鹏 译) ★★★★

4. A long journey tests a horse's stamina; a long time reveals a man's heart.

(石爱伟 译) ★●●

5. Distance tests a horse's power, and time tells a man's heart.

(张俊锋 译1) ★●●

6. Time is a great revealer of human nature.

(王昌玲 译1) ★★★

7. A long ride tests a steed's vigor; a long time tells a man's nature.

(石永浩 译) ●●●

8. Distance tests horse power; time tells human nature.

(王绍昌 译) ●●●

9. Distance tests a horse's strength; time tells a person's loyalty.

(任诚刚 译) ●●●

10. Distance test the power of a steed, and time a man's heart reads.

(张俊锋 译2) ★●

11. Distance proves a horse's stamina, time shows one's true heart.

(叶如钢 译1) ★★

12. Long journeys show the horse is strong; getting on for long proves one's wrong.

(魏红霞 译) ●●

13. Only after a long distance running can we tell the strength of a horse; only after a long time together can we know the truth of friendship.

(冯雷 译) ●●

14. As time goes, human true nature shows.

(王昌玲 译2) ★

15. Distance challenges stamina, and time reveals integrity.

（樊功生 译）★

16. A long journey proves a horse's strength, a long time reveals a man's heart.

（叶如钢 译2）★

【163】年光似鸟翩翩过，世事如棋局局新。

——释志文《西阁》

投票：外方评委7人投票★，中方评委4人投票●

1. Time flies and circumstances change.

（王毅 译）★★★★●

2. Time flies by like birds passing with no sound, the world changes as chess does, shifting every round.

（杨胜悦 译）★●●●

3. Time hastens itself as in bird glides; world renews itself as in chess rounds.

（王绍昌 译）●●●

4. Years lightly fly away like birds; events unfold like games of chess.

（吴春晓 译）★●

5. Time flies like a bird, and things change like a chess game.

（王成杰 译）●●

6. Time flies and the world changes.

（田璐 译）★

7. Time flies, like the bird across the skyline; things change, like every game of chess.

（魏红霞 译）★

8. Time flies as swiftly as a bird, and the world changes as unpredictably as every new game of chess.

（张晓阳 译）★

9. The elapse of time is as fast as flying birds. Like playing board games, in spite of losing at the first, we still have the chance to win.

（王婷 译）★

第三篇　唐宋时期

第四篇
元明清时期

Chapter IV
Yuan，Ming，and Qing Dynasties

【164】人生万事须自为，跬步江山即寥廓。

——范梈《王氏能远楼》

投票：外方评委7人投票★，中方评委4人投票●

1. Spare no effort to get things done and you will step into a vast world.

（王成杰 译）★★★★●

2. Be self-reliant in life and one can go far with each small step forward.

（王毅 译）★★★●

3. All things in life should be done by ourselves；each small step we take leads to a whole wide world.

（马建军 译）●●●●

4. Rely on yourself for optimal results.

（陶家乐 译）★★★

5. Take charge for everything，and the whole world opens up with tiny steps.

（樊功生 译）★●

6. You've got to take concrete action in person；step by step，you will scale a high mountain.

（王昌玲 译）★★

7. Dare to live the life you have dreamed for yourself. Each step forward will open for you a new horizon.

（王如利 译）★★

8. It is a must for us to do all things in life by ourselves. Even half a pace forward at a time，keep going and we will enter a vast splendid world.

（倪庆行 译）●●

9. Perseverance makes success，striving step by step brings a broad world.

（郁序新 译）★

名言警句英译

10. Through thick and thin we all have to walk the way of our own, for every single step helps us get to the land of Canaan.

（乐国斌 译）★

【165】画虎画皮难画骨，知人知面不知心。

——孟汉卿《张孔目智勘魔合罗》

投票：外方评委5人投票★，中方评委8人投票●

1. You can paint a tiger and its skin, but not its bones. You may know the man and his appearance, but not always his mind.

（樊功生 译）★★★●●●●

2. Knowing a person's soul is as hard as painting a tiger's bones.

（史红霞 译）★●●●●

3. It's easy to draw a tiger's skin but hard to draw its bones, and it's easy to know a person's face but hard to fathom his mind.

（张晓阳 译1）★●●●

4. A tiger's bones are harder to draw than skin, a man's heart is harder to know than face.

（叶如钢 译）★★★★

5. Cats hide their claws, and people hide their minds.

（张晓阳 译2，cats hide their claws 为俚语借鉴）●●●●

6. One can only paint the shape of a tiger, but never penetrate its fur to reach the bone. Similarly, one can recognize a man by his face, but never know whether his heart is in the right place.

（王昌玲 译）★★●

7. As a tiger's bone is hard to draw, a man's heart is hard to know.

（丁立群 译）★●●

8. In drawing a tiger, you may draw its skin, but not its bones; in knowing a person, you may read his face, but not his mind.

（王绍昌 译1）★●●

9. Easier to draw a tiger's fur than to draw its bone; easier to know a man's face than to know his heart.

（王毅 译）●●●

10. Just as a tiger's bones are not easy to paint as its skin, a man's heart is not easy to learn as his face.

（冯雷 译）●●●

11. It's easy to paint the likeness of a tiger or a portrait of a person; it's difficult to probe into the tiger's bones or the person's heart.

（石爱伟 译）★●

12. It's easy to sketch or match the exteriors but difficult to patch or catch the interiors.

（王绍昌 译2）★●

【166】不要人夸好颜色，只留清气满乾坤。

——王冕《墨梅·其三》

投票：外方评委 4 人投票★，中方评委 6 人投票●

1. The freshness of a flower fades fast, yet the quality of the freshness will last.

（冯雷 译）★★★●●

2. The plums seek not praises for their colors. Instead, they prefer their aromas spread all over.

（王绍昌 译）★●●●

3. Ink Plum never wishes to be acclaimed for its good appearance, but to permeate the whole world with its pure fragrance.

（张俊锋 译）●●●●

4. The plums don't need boasting of their color; the whole world is full of their aroma.

（魏红霞 译）★●●

5. Do not praise its good color, people only admire its charming fragrance to leave in the whole world.

（任诚刚 译）★●●

6. Colors are dazzling but easy to fade; fragrance is out of sight but nothing can hide.

（李开林 译1）★●●

7. A plum tree's spring petals depicted by delicate color may attract viewers to flatter. But what prevails is its refreshing fragrance of faith brewed in winter though it's behind the paper.

（李开林 译2）★●●

8. No laud for colors they try to procure, they just pervade the world with fragrance pure.

（石永浩 译）●●

9. Its fine color needs no praises. Its noble scent fills all places.

（叶如钢 译）●●

10. Expect not people's praise of my beautiful color, but permeate my fragrance far and wide.

（倪庆行 译）★

11. Desirous of none's praise for the luster, except leaving scent to perfume the air.

（王昌玲 译）★

【167】 人之聪明，多失于浮炫。——《金史·列传·卷三十三》

投票：外方评委8人投票★，中方评委7人投票●

1. Vanity blunts one's intelligence.

（冯雷 译）★★●●●

2. Much wisdom can be lost in vanity.

（任诚刚 译）★★★

3. A man's wisdom is often lost to his ego.

（杨胜悦 译）★★★

4. People's shrewdness is often sabotaged by their ostentation.

（倪庆行 译）●●●

5. A smart person always outsmarts himself by flaunt and vanity.

（王毅 译）●●●

6. Ostentatiousness often eats away wisdom.

（王梅兰 译）●●●

7. Be quick to think and react, but be slow to show off your achievements.

（吴春晓 译）★★

8. A man will lose his wit when he is boastful and flaunting.

（杨中仁 译）★★

9. One is often too showy to be wise.

（王成杰 译）●●

10. One's intelligence is easily lost in ostentation.

（田璐 译）●●

11. A common flaw in one's cleverness is the habitual craving for showing off.

（李开林 译）★

【168】运用之妙，存乎一心。——《宋史·岳飞传》

投票：外方评委7人投票★，中方评委3人投票●

1. Careful and logical considerations determine effective and flexible strategies and tactics.

（郁序新 译）★★★★★●

2. The art of application and manipulation lies in the mind.

（张俊锋 译）★★★

3. The clever use of tactics consists in clear thinking.

（何艳 译）★●

4. The art of command lies in flexibility.

（丁如伟 译）★●

5. A good commander issues orders according to the actual situation.

（王毅 译）★★

6. Ingenious and flexible application of a stratagem lies in the commander's sound judgement and originality.

（石爱伟 译）●●

7. A tactic can only bring great success if employed smartly.

（叶如钢 译）★

8. The key to a practice lies in the mind.

（田璐 译）★

【169】有缘千里来相会，无缘对面不相逢。

——施耐庵《水浒传》

1. It isn't distance but destiny that ties a couple together or stops their encounter.

（杨中仁 译）★★★★★★★●

2. Some are destined to meet even if they are thousand miles apart; some are doomed to be strangers even if they walk side by side.

（石爱伟 译）★★●●●●●

3. If predestined, we will meet even if we are a long way apart; if not, one hundred face-to-face encounters won't stir our heart.

（冯雷 译）●●●●

4. We meet or miss someone by fate.

（彭智鹏 译）●●●

5. We may meet and cling to each other though living myriad miles apart; we may often see and pass by each other yet remaining strangers.

（石永浩 译）★●

6. Love is a real magic that can attract two strangers far away to date together; if no love, they will miss each other even very near.

（郁序新 译）●●

7. Where there is fate, there is date. No fate, no date.

（赵宜忠 译） ● ●

8. Soul mates, regardless of thousands of miles apart, are bound to meet and unite in marriage. Utter strangers, even encountered face to face, are utter strangers without any change.

（倪庆行 译） ★

9. With a bond heaven-sent, two people far apart shall meet at last; without it, they are simply strangers even though they are face to face.

（铁冰 译） ★

【170】 玉可碎而不可改其白，竹可焚而不可毁其节。

——罗贯中《三国演义》第七十六回

投票：外方评委 8 人投票★，中方评委 5 人投票●

1. Smashed jade retains its color; burnt bamboo keeps its character.

（乐国斌 译） ★ ★ ★ ★ ●

2. Jade may be crumbled, but remains white; bamboo may be burnt, but stays upright.

（叶如钢 译1） ★ ★ ★ ★

3. Jade can be smashed but its true color never fades away; bamboo can be burnt but its uprightness in people's mind does stay.

（冯雷 译1） ● ● ● ●

4. Jade can be broken but its spotless nature can't be changed; bamboo can be burnt but its upright character can't be changed.

（魏红霞 译） ★ ★ ●

5. Jade can be broken but not changed in its white purity; bamboo can be burnt but not destroyed in its integrity.

（任诚刚 译）●●●

6. Broken jade can remain white; burnt bamboo can remain upright.

（王绍昌 译）★●

7. Jade forever remains white, even being crumbled; bamboo joints never give in, even being burnt.

（叶如钢 译2）★★

8. Even broken, jade its purity retains; even burned, the uprightness of bamboo remains.

（王昌玲 译）●●

9. A broken jade remains true to its pureness; a burnt bamboo is remembered for its uprightness.

（冯雷 译2）●●

10. Jade smashed keeps its color; bamboo burnt maintains its character.

（曹小菁 译）●●

【171】心狭为祸之根，心旷为福之门。——王阳明《传习录》

投票：外方评委10人投票★，中方评委4人投票●

1. One's frame of mind determines one's destiny.

（叶步青 译）★★★★★★★★●

2. Narrow-mindedness invites bad luck, while broad-mindedness brings good fortune.

（张莹 译）●●●●

3. Narrow-mindedness is the root of misfortune and broad-mindedness is the key to happiness.

（史红霞 译）★●●

4. One's degree of tolerance decides his destiny.

（曹小菁 译）★★★

5. Narrow-mindedness is the root of disasters, while open-mindedness is the door towards auspiciousness.

（倪庆行 译）●●●

6. Narrow-minded, he'll sow the seed of disaster; broad-minded, he'll open the door to good fortune.

（魏红霞 译）★●

7. Woe befalls the narrow-minded, and blessed are the broad-minded.

（王成杰 译）●●

8. The narrow-minded bring troubles, and the open-minded blessings.

（刘向军 译）●●

9. A narrow mind leads one to ruin; a broad mind guides one to gain.

（王毅 译）★

10. Misfortune often comes to the narrow-minded, while happiness to the broad-minded.

（马建军 译）★

11. One's narrow thought is the root of the disaster; broad mind has the door opened for the blessing.

（任诚刚 译）★

12. A selfish heart is misfortune's root, enrichment is a giving heart's fruit.

（杨胜悦 译）★

13. The door of happiness opens to generous hearts, the door of disaster to mean ones.

（杨秀波 译）★

【172】 破山中贼易，破心中贼难。

——王阳明《与杨仕德薛尚谦书》

投票：外方评委6人投票★，中方评委4人投票●

1. It's easier to subdue the demon in the mountain than that in the heart.

（王毅 译）★★●●●

2. It's harder to overcome demons than to storm a castle.

（王成杰 译）★★★●

3. Evil deeds will be easily brought to justice, but evil thoughts are always at large.

（吴春晓 译）★★●●

4. Demons in the woods are easy to defeat. Demons in the spirit are hard to dispel.

（张晔 译）●●●

5. It's easier to defeat the enemy in the real world than the dark side in one's heart.

（董秀静 译）★●

6. What stole one's heart is the hardest to defeat.

（曹小菁 译）★

7. It is easier to defeat the thieves in the mountains than foes in the heart.

（任诚刚 译）●

8. True victory lies in winning the enemies' heart, not their mere surrender of arms.

（刘向军 译）●

9. It's easier to subdue evil-doers hidden in the hills than to curb evil thoughts in people's hearts.

（石爱伟 译）●

名言警句英译

10. It's easier to beat the bandits gathered in a mountain than to banish the evil thoughts lodged in the heart.

（杨中仁 译）●

【173】志于道德者，功名不足累其心；志于功名者，富贵不足以累其心。

——王阳明《与黄诚甫书》

投票：外方评委 5 人投票★，中方评委 2 人投票●

1. It is the purpose that finally decides one's concern.

（杨秀波 译）★★★★

2. A man for morality won't trouble himself for fame; a man for fame won't trouble himself for wealth.

（杨中仁 译）★●

3. Morality brings people inner peace, whereas fame brings them mental burden.

（张晓阳 译）★

4. A man pursuing virtue remains indifferent to fame. A man seeking fame keeps unconcerned about wealth.

（伍敏毓 译）★

5. If a person is determined to cultivate morality, he has no regard for fame and fortune; if a person aspires to fame and fortune, he doesn't think about wealth and prosperity.

（邢珽 译）●

6. If one strives for virtues, one's heart won't be troubled by fame. If one strives for fame, one's heart won't be troubled by wealth and status.

（叶如钢 译）●

7. People pursuing ethics and morals are never troubled by honors and fames. People chasing honors and fames are never haunted by riches and titles.

（王绍昌 译）●

8. To those who are dedicated to virtue, meritorious service is negligible; to those who are dedicated to meritorious service, wealth and rank are out of their mind.

（乐国斌 译）●

9. One who seeks moral principles doesn't care about fame, and one who seeks fame doesn't care about wealth.

（马建军 译）●

10. Those who aspire to moral cultivation do not care about high social rank; those who aspire to high social rank do not care about riches.

（何艳 译）●

11. Cherishing lofty ideals, one will not be obsessed with rank or glory; pursuing rank or glory, one will not be crazy for wealth or nobility.

（石永浩 译）●

【174】静坐常思自己过，闲谈莫论他人非。

——罗状元《罗状元醒世歌》

投票：外方评委11人投票★，中方评委6人投票●

1. Meditate and examine yourself rather than gossip and criticize others.

（田璐 译）★★★★★★★★★★●

名言警句英译

2. Be self-reflective when alone; gossip not when in company.

（王成杰 译）★★●●●

3. Beware of your own weaknesses and learn from others' strengths.

（刘向军 译）★★★★

4. Better to examine your own faults, but not to gossip about others' shortcomings.

（杨中仁 译）●●●

5. Repent often while alone, never gossip on others.

（樊功生 译）●●●

6. More introspecting, no backbiting.

（石永浩 译）●●●

7. Reflect on your mistakes when alone, but refrain from criticizing others when in company.

（马建军 译）★●

8. In solitude, ponder often upon one's own faults; in conversation, talk only about one's own business.

（王梅兰 译）★★

9. Reflect on yourself and don't discuss other people.

（冯雷 译）★★

10. Reflecting on yourself is good, while gossiping is not.

（陶家乐 译）★★

11. Reflect on your own faults in meditation; never scandalize others in conversation.

（王昌玲 译）●●

12. Ponder over my own faults but never chat about others' rights or wrongs.

（魏红霞 译）●●

【175】物忌全盛，事忌全美，人忌全名。

——吕坤《呻吟语·修身篇》

投票：外方评委6人投票★，中方评委6人投票●

1. Perfect things don't last long；long-lasting things aren't perfect.

（冯雷 译）★●●●

2. Any success contains failure，and any perfection contains deficiency. It is impossible to be hundred percent perfect for everything or everyone.

（郁序新 译）★★★★

3. Imperfection is the norm of life.

（吴春晓 译）★★●

4. Whatever you're doing，seek no perfection. Perfection is beginning of deterioration.

（王昌玲 译）★●●

5. It is perilous for lives to be too exuberant，for things to be too perfect，or for men to be too reputed.

（叶如钢 译）●●●

6. Don't go to extremes in everything.

（马建军 译）★●

7. Nothing can be 100% perfect.

（马金龙 译）★●

8. Never seek the supreme splendor in objects，the permanent peak in matters，and the full fame in men.

（王绍昌 译）●●

9. Better happily live with defects than painfully seek to be perfect.

（石永浩 译）●●

名言警句英译

【176】风声雨声读书声声声入耳；家事国事天下事事事关心。

——顾宪成　东林书院门前对联

投票：外方评委7人投票★，中方评委2人投票●

1. The whistling wind, the pelting rain and the sound of reading are pleasant to the ears. The affairs about the family, the state and the world are on the scholar's mind.

（王昌玲 译）★★★●

2. Hearing the wind blowing, the rain falling, and students reading aloud, we're concerned about our family, our nation, and the world affairs.

（魏红霞 译）★★★

3. The sounds of wind, rain and reading aloud are all pleasant to my ears; the affairs of family, state and the world are all dear to my heart.

（马建军 译）★●

4. What I enjoy are the pleasant sounds of wind, rain and reading. What I care about are the affairs of family, state and human being.

（张晓阳 译）★●

5. The wind and the rain accompany the students' reading. The state and the world affairs galvanize their concerns.

（吴春晓 译）★★

6. Students should be concerned with minor as well as major affairs ranging from family to state and listen not only to the chanting of classics but also sound of live nature.

（石爱伟 译）★

7. Breeze, drizzle and book reading constantly come to my ears. Home, country and world affairs frequently flow to my mind.

（张立国 译）★

8. Listen consciously to the rain, to the wind, and to the sound of reading. Show great concern for your family, for your country, and for the whole wide world.

（何冰 译）★

9. The sound of wind, rain and reading are both harmonious and pleasant. The matter of one's family, country and the world all concern a highly responsible person.

（杨秀波 译）★

10. Take the sound of wind, rain and reading into ears and put family, national and global affairs into mind.

（董秀静 译）★

【177】读万卷书，行万里路。——董其昌《画禅室随笔》

投票：外方评委3人投票★，中方评委6人投票●

1. Reading abundantly as well as travelling widely makes a powerful lear-ner.

（艾朝阳 译）●●●●●●

2. Reading broadens the mind, travel opens the eyes.

（叶如钢 译）★★●

3. A well-read traveller sees the world.

（彭智鹏 译）★●●

4. Extensive reading broadens perceptions; distant travels extends perspec-tives.

（王绍昌 译）★●●

名言警句英译

5. Read myriad books and travel myriad miles.

（张俊锋 译）●●●

6. Do read more, score much more; do travel more, find much more.

（郁序新 译1）●●●

7. Read much and travel more, then your vision will be broad.

（曹小菁 译）●●●

8. Read extensively to widen your horizons; travel widely to broaden your vision.

（石永浩 译）★●

9. Read abundantly, travel extensively.

（樊功生 译）★●

10. One can lead a full life by reading ten thousand books and traveling ten thousand miles.

（刘群 译）★●

11. Read and travel more, and you will acquire knowledge galore.

（倪庆行 译）●●

12. More books make you think deeper; more trips make you sight wider.

（郁序新 译2）●●

13. Read as much as possible; travel as far as possible!

（王昌玲 译）★

14. Reading opens your mind; traveling opens your eyes.

（张琼 译）★

【178】先淡后浓，先疏后亲，先远后近，交友道也。

——陈继儒《小窗幽记·集醒篇》

投票：外方评委 11 人投票★，中方评委 6 人投票●

1. True friendship develops slowly and takes long to build.

（冯雷 译1）★ ★ ★ ★ ★ ★ ★ ●

2. The way to forge true friendship is to undergo an indispensable process,
one from weak to strong, from aloof to intimate and from distant to close.

（倪庆行 译）★ ● ● ● ● ●

3. Natural friendship develops from shallow to deep, from distant to close.

（乐国斌 译）★ ★ ★ ★ ●

4. Friendship develops as the relationship becomes stronger, denser, and
closer.

（曹小菁 译）★ ★ ★ ●

5. It takes long to cultivate deep and strong friendships.

（王绍昌 译）★ ★ ★ ★

6. How would friendship last long? It starts thin, distant and weak, then
comes thick, close and strong.

（冯雷 译2）● ● ● ●

7. Bland, sparse and remote first, and strong, dense, and close later, this is
the way for friendships to grow.

（叶如钢 译）● ● ●

8. Thick after thin, dense after sparse, near after far, that's the way to make
friends.

（任诚刚 译）● ● ●

9. It takes time and tact to build up strong friendships that last. There is no
rush in it.

（王昌玲 译）★ ★

名言警句英译

10. The supposed way to develop friendship is to evolve it with time and distance.

（李开林 译）●●

11. The very way toward friendship is to keep a relationship tenuous, alienated and distant first while strong, intimate and close later.

（段冰知 译）●●

12. The arts of making friends lies in the gradual shortening of the distance.

（程永生 译）★

13. Friendship arrives like a train, warms like a heater, and grows like a tree.

（艾朝阳 译）★

14. Friendship grows stronger, deeper and more intimate naturally, such being the right way of making friends.

（石永浩 译）★

【179】闭门即是深山，读书随处净土。

——陈继儒《小窗幽记·集灵篇》

投票：外方评委6人投票★，中方评委7人投票●

1. By closing the door, you shut the noises out; by opening a book, your spiritual world sprouts.

（冯雷 译1）★★★★★●●

2. A closed door: serenity; an opened book: purity.

（王昌玲 译）★★●●●

3. Close your door and you enjoy solitude of a deep mountain; open your book and you find serenity of a pure land.

（石永浩 译）●●●●●

4. A room with door shut makes an isolated world; absorption in reading creates a spiritual land.

（冯雷 译2）★★●●

5. Shutting my door, I live a hermit's life; reading my books, I live in my dream paradise.

（铁冰 译）●●●

6. If you close the door, you won't be disturbed as if you're living in the mountains; if you read books, your mind will be purified as if you're living in the paradise.

（魏红霞 译1）●●●

7. A closed door quiets down the yard; an open book comforts the heart.

（李开林 译）●●●

8. Hidden behind closed doors, you are secluded as in deep mountains; reading between open pages, you are immersed as in pure land.

（王绍昌 译）●●●

9. Close the door, you won't be disturbed; read books, your mind will be purified.

（魏红霞 译2）★●

10. Closing the room door induces quietness of deep mounts, and reading a book brings one into divine land.

（叶如钢 译）●●

11. Closing the door drives out vanity, and reading a book brings in purity.

（瞿琼学 译1）●●

12. When the door is close, a room can be a serene mountain; when a book is opened, any place can turn into a wonderland.

（刘群 译）★

13. Closing the door secludes one in mountains. Reading a book immerses one in paradise.

（瞿琼学 译2）★

【180】喜时之言多失信，怒时之言多失体。

——陈继儒《小窗幽记·集法篇》

投票：外方评委9人投票★，中方评委4人投票●

1. Be careful with your words in the heat of the moment.

（王成杰 译）★★★★★★★★★●

2. Never take the words seriously from a person wild with joy or mad with anger.

（冯雷 译）★★●●●

3. An excited man often makes big-mouth promises; an angry man often says inappropriate words.

（石爱伟 译）●●

4. Words said in excitement are always untrustworthy; words said in anger are always inappropriate.

（王毅 译）●●

5. What we say in an ecstasy is often unreliable, and inappropriate in a fury.

（马建军 译）★

6. Words in pleasure are often not reliable, and those in anger mostly not elegant.

（杨秀波 译）★

7. A man's remark tends to be unreliable when he is ecstatic, and inappropriate when angry.

（刘向军 译）●

8. Do not let your heart meddle with your tongue. Always speak truthfully and decently.

（吴春晓 译）●

9. Happy promises are easily broken; angry curses are indecently spoken.

（王昌玲 译）●

10. Being overjoyed leads you to break your word easily. Anger makes you fail to express yourself properly.

（张立国 译）●

11. Word given in delight is scarcely kept; words said in anger are barely elegant.

（丁如伟 译）●

12. Words uttered in anger lack credit; words uttered in joys lack propriety.

（王绍昌 译）●

13. An ecstatic man tends to talk big. An angry man easily speaks something rude.

（田璐 译）●

14. Words in joy may lose faith; words in rage may lose face.

（崔传明 译）●

【181】士人有百折不回之真心，才有万变不穷之妙用。

——陈继儒《小窗幽记·集峭篇》

投票：外方评委7人投票★，中方评委3人投票●

1. Perseverance is the secret of all triumphs.

（马建军 译）★★★★★●

2. Those who persevere are the ones who succeed.

（陶家乐 译）★★★★

3. A true man builds resilience to solve problems under various circumstances.

（王梅兰 译）●●●●

4. He who remains true to himself despite twists and turns will be able to cope with changes and challenges.

（刘雪芹 译）★●●

5. The true nature of a determined heart is capable of coping with all sorts of changing situations.

（石爱伟 译）★●

6. Determination and perseverance can make one successful in everything.

（丁如伟 译）★●

7. As long as one has a strong will to keep pushing forward despite repeated frustrations, he can acquire the ability to conquer all difficulties.

（董秀静 译）★★

8. The indomitable take adversity in stride.

（王成杰 译）★

9. A man with an iron will can thrive in any situations.

（樊功生 译）★

10. Only after having endured can you succeed.

（杨胜悦 译）★

11. Indomitable fortitude gets one anywhere he wants.

（王毅 译）★

12. A person who remains faithful and unyielding is able to encounter the vicissitudes of the world with ingenuity.

（何艳 译）★

【182】 刻薄不赚钱，忠厚不折本。——冯梦龙《醒世恒言》

投票：外方评委6人投票★，中方评委6人投票●

1. Kindness rewards, while meanness does the opposite.

（石永浩 译）★●●●●

2. Be kind and generous, and you'll be treated the same way in return.

（刘向军 译）★★★★★

3. Blessed are the kind-hearted; cursed are the evil-minded.

（王成杰 译1）★★★●

4. It pays to be honest.

（马建军 译）★●●

5. Being mean brings you no profit and being kind costs you no penny.

（王梅兰 译）●●●

6. Honesty is the best business policy.

（王绍昌 译，借用英语谚语）●●●

7. The god of wealth favors the honest, not the mean.

（王成杰 译2）★●

8. Meanness brings one no gain; honesty makes one no loss.

（丁如伟 译）●●

9. Kindness causes no losses to one just as meanness produces no profits for him/her.

（王毅 译）★

【183】将在谋而不在勇，兵在精而不在多。

——冯梦龙《古今小说》

投票：外方评委7人投票★，中方评委4人投票●

1. For commanders, wisdom weighs more than courage. For soldiers, quality matters more than quantity.

（王梅兰 译）★★★★★●●●

2. Brain rather than brawn makes a general; quality rather than quantity makes a troop.

（王成杰 译）★●●●●

3. Strategy over bravery, quality over quantity.

（陶家乐 译）★★★★

4. For a general, what really counts is not his courage but his strategy. For a troop, what really counts is not its quantity but its quality.

（倪庆行 译）★●●

5. What makes a good general is his strategy, not bravery; what makes a good army is not the number, but the quality of the soldiers.

（马百亮 译）★●●

6. It is not the courage, but the strategy that makes a general. It is not the quantity, but the excellence that makes a troop.

（张立国 译）★●

7. A general's bravery is not so important as his tactics, nor is the quantity of soldiers as the quality of them.

（张晓阳 译）★

8. For a general, strategy is more important than mere valor; for an army, strength is preferred to mere number.

（石爱伟 译）★

9. A general's strategy is prized above bravery; the soldiers' ability to combat matters more than their number.

（何艳 译）★

10. Competency of a leader lies in his tactics rather than bravery. Strength of a team lies in the qualifications of the staff rather than numbers.

（何冰 译）★

11. A general's success depends on his resourcefulness rather than his courage and a troop's success depends on the strength rather than the number of its soldiers.

（董秀静 译）★

【184】大厦之成，非一木之材也；大海之阔，非一流之归也。

——冯梦龙《东周列国志》

投票：外方评委 8 人投票★，中方评委 3 人投票●

1. One single log doesn't make a cabin; one single stream doesn't achieve the immensity of a sea.

（石爱伟 译）★★★★

2. A grand edifice is not built of a single timber; a vast sea is not fed by a single river.

(倪庆行 译) ★●●

3. A grand mansion isn't built with only a single log; a vast ocean isn't amassed from just one tributary.

(樊功生 译) ★●●

4. One log builds no mansion, one stream makes no sea. Gathering is the key.

(刘德江 译) ★★★

5. A large building is made of many planks; an ocean is made of many streams.

(瑞雪 译) ★★★

6. A big mansion is not built of one single log. A vast ocean is not formed by one lone stream.

(王如利 译) ★●

7. One log cannot make a gigantic mansion; one brook cannot make a boundless ocean.

(王昌玲 译) ★●

8. A mansion cannot be built from the wood of a single tree; the vastness of the sea cannot be formed by a single river.

(任诚刚 译) ★★

9. One log cannot make a mansion. One drop cannot make the ocean.

(马百亮 译) ★

10. Just as no building can be built relying on the wood from one tree, the flow of a single river can never form the vastness of the sea.

(张晓阳 译) ★

11. A big mansion is not built of a single piece of timber; a vast ocean is not formed by a single river.

(马建军 译) ★

12. The wood from one tree is not enough to build a large building; the water from one river is not enough to form a vast ocean.

（冯雷 译）★

13. No grandeur of a tower is built on the timber of one tree; no vastness of an ocean is formed with the flow of one river.

（石永浩 译）★

14. Many a little makes a mickle; many a mickle makes a miracle.

（崔传明 译）★

【185】留得青山在，不怕没柴烧。

——凌濛初《初刻拍案惊奇》

投票：外方评委11人投票★，中方评委7人投票●

1. Wherever humans survive, hopes forever thrive.

（王绍昌 译）★★★★★★★★★●

2. "Where there is life, there is hope."

（郁序新 译）★★★★★★★●●

3. As long as the hill is green in spring, there will be plenty of firewood in winter.

（石爱伟 译）★★★★★★★●

4. As long as the green mountains still stand, who worries about the shortage of firewood?

（张晓阳 译）★★★★★●

5. Green hills make firewood available; survived people make future possible.

（丁如伟 译）●●●●●●

6. Where there is a life, there is a hope.

(杨中仁 译1,借用网络译文) ★●●●●

7. Survival means hope.

(樊功生 译) ●●●●

8. As long as mountains are green, one worries less about firewood.

(杨中仁 译2) ★★★

9. As the existence of green mountain would spare your worry of firewood shortage, the state of being alive would endow you with hope for future success.

(王毅 译) ●●●

10. Whenever the green mountain exists, there is no need to worry about firewood.

(杨秀波 译) ●●●

11. There always exists hope as long as there is life.

(史红霞 译) ★●

12. With green hills there, no worries about firewood. With life there, there's always hope.

(董庆瑗 译) ●●

【186】 德从宽处积，福向俭中求。——王时敏　自题联

投票：外方评委5人投票★，中方评委4人投票●

1. Being tolerant strengthens one's virtue. Living a simple life grows happiness.

(何冰 译) ★★★★●

2. Forgiveness is the fountainhead of virtues; thrift is the cornucopia of blessings.

（吴春晓 译）★●●●

3. Virtue grows from tolerance; happiness stems from frugality.

（马建军 译）★●●●

4. Tolerance enriches morality; prudence drives happiness.

（王梅兰 译）★●●

5. Virtue lies in lenience and kindness, happiness thrift and simplicity.

（杨中仁 译）★★

6. Virtues are based on generosity; wealth is built through frugality.

（叶如钢 译）●●

7. Virtues spring from tolerance; blessings stem from frugality.

（王绍昌 译）●●

8. To make merit, be generous with people; to seek blessing, live a simple life.

（王成杰 译）★

9. Virtue comes from an open mind; fortune comes from a fastened wallet.

（杨胜悦 译）★

【187】志高则言洁，志大则辞弘，志远则旨永。

——叶燮《原诗·外篇上》

投票：外方评委 5 人投票★，中方评委 3 人投票●

1. Words of men with lofty goals are elegant, writings of men with grand goals magnificent, and tenets of men with far-reaching goals long-lasting.

（叶如钢 译）★●●

2. Lofty aspirations deepen a writer's insight, purify his language and improve his rhetoric.

(冯雷 译) ★●

3. A lofty man writes clearly, an ambitious man powerfully, and a visionary man profoundly.

(王如利 译) ★●

4. Noble verses may come from aiming high, eloquence from dreaming big, profoundness from thinking far.

(樊功生 译) ★★

5. The nature of a person's aspirations determines the nature of their works.

(杨胜悦 译) ★★

6. For those with noble aspirations, their works are elegant in wording; with big aspirations, vigorous in style; with lofty aspirations, profound in thought.

(马建军 译) ●●

7. Sky-high inspirations cultivate cleanness in speech; cosmic inspirations generate grandness in diction; far-ranging inspirations create permanence of purpose.

(王绍昌 译) ●●

8. The elegant writes in a pure way, the aspirational in a magnificent way, and the ambitious in a profound way.

(张晓阳 译) ★

9. People with lofty aspirations will write concisely; people with great ambitions will write vigorously; people with high aims will write thought-provokingly.

(倪庆行 译) ★

10. He who has a lofty ideal writes concisely, forcefully, and profoundly.

(王昌玲 译) ★

11. Moral people live a clean life; big hearts talk about one love; futurists cares for eternity.

（孙玲玲 译）★

12. Themes and expression must match. Themes can be described as lofty, grand or didactic and expressions should be chosen accordingly, for example, concise, flowery, or logical.

（石爱伟 译）★

13. Lofty ideals give rise to concise and eloquent expressions, and profound thoughts.

（何艳 译）★

14. If a poet cherishes lofty ideals, his poems tend to be lucid and vigorous in style, with profound thought flowing between the lines.

（石永浩 译）★

【188】宜未雨而绸缪，毋临渴而掘井。

——朱柏庐《朱子家训》

投票：外方评委 8 人投票★，中方评委 2 人投票●

1. Repair your house before the rain falls; dig a well before you get thirsty.
（石爱伟 译）★★★★★★★

2. It's better to prepare for a rain to come than hasten to cope with it after it comes, just as better to dig a well before a drought than after it.

（艾朝阳 译）★★★●

3. Better repair your roof before the rain; when you are thirsty, digging a well will be in vain.

（王昌玲 译）★★★●

4. Be prepared in advance for the unforeseen; it's too late to think about wells when thirsty.

（樊功生 译）★★●●

5. Do prepare for foul in fair weather; when thirsty, it's too late to be a well-digger.

（郁序新 译）★★★★

6. Witty to reinforce your house before the rainstorm; silly to dig a well after you're thirsty.

（魏红霞 译）★★●

7. Repair the roof and dig a well before it is too late; waiting is a mistake.

（冯雷 译）★●●

8. Fix roof leaks before it rains, and dig a well before being compelled by thirst.

（叶如钢 译）★●

9. It's as late to fix the roof when the rain is falling as to dig a well when your throat is burning with thirst.

（石爱伟 译）★★

【189】宠辱不惊，闲看庭前花开花落；去留无意，漫随天外云卷云舒。

——洪应明《菜根谭》

投票：外方评委7人投票★，中方评委4人投票●

1. Remaining indifferent to honor or disgrace, I leisurely watch the flowers blooming and fading in front of the court; caring nothing about demotion or promotion, I calmly appreciate the clouds rolling and extending in the sky.

（张晓阳 译）★★●●

2. Gains and losses are like flowers blooming and withering; ups and downs are like clouds gathering and scattering.

（王成杰 译）★ ★ ★ ★

3. Undisturbed by favor or dishonor, leisurely one looks at the flowers that bloom and fade before the pavilion. Unmindful of leaving or staying, freely one watches the clouds that gather and spread in the sky.

（何艳 译）★ ★ ●

4. Favored or humiliated, a magnanimous man won't be startled and he will leisurely gaze at the flowers that either come out or fall in front of the court yard. Placed or displaced, an open-minded man will show no concern and he will watch the clouds in the sky curling and spreading with ease.

（倪庆行 译）● ● ●

5. Don't place much importance on glory or humiliation, which are like the garden flowers blooming and falling. Don't place much importance on promotion or demotion, which are like the clouds gathering and dispersing.

（杨中仁 译）★ ●

6. Never be bothered by glory or shame, which is as normal as flowers bloom or fade away; nor be troubled by staying or leaving, which is as natural as clouds gather or drift apart.

（冯雷 译）★ ●

7. Don't be disturbed if favored or fall out of grace, like flowers at yard blooming and falling at ease. Don't be mindful if promoted or removed from posts, like clouds in sky gathering and dispersing at will.

（王绍昌 译）● ●

8. Not stunned at fame or shame, I leisurely watch the flowers budding and fading. Not worried about leave or stay, I randomly follow the clouds floating and flowing.

（崔传明 译）● ●

9. Favour or disgrace, remain undisturbed. To leave or to stay, neither is planned. Flowers bloom and fade, my eyes beheld. Clouds gather and diffuse, my heart followed.

（田璐 译）●●

10. When dealing with another person's affairs, you should be calm and collected. When going through gains and dips in one's personal life, one should act in a balanced manner.

（陶家乐 译）★

11. Go with the flow.

（杨胜悦 译）★

12. Keep calm with honor and dishonor, gain and loss. Thus one can have the mood for appreciating the flowers in the courtyard and the clouds in the sky.

（董秀静 译）★

【190】不责人小过，不发人阴私，不念人旧恶。

——洪应明《菜根谭》

投票：外方评委9人投票★，中方评委4人投票●

1. Don't blame someone for small mistakes, don't reveal other's secrets, don't always bring up another person's past faults.

（陶家乐 译）★★★●●

2. Do not blame people for their minor demerits, do not expose their shameful secrets, and do not be preoccupied with old grievances.

（倪庆行 译）★★★●

3. Don't chastise a person for small errors, don't air out their private affairs, don't constantly recall their old mistakes.

（杨胜悦 译）★★★

4. Don't blame others for their small mistakes, don't disclose others' privacy and don't bear in mind others' unfriendly treatment to you in the past.

（董秀静 译）★★★

5. Don't blame others for minor mistakes, don't expose other people's privacy, and don't harbor bad feelings for past offences.

（马百亮 译）★●

6. Do not reveal others' scars at will.

（郁序新 译）★●

7. Don't find fault with others, don't expose their privacy, and let go of old grudges.

（马建军 译）★●

8. Don't blame one for minor errors, don't disclose one's privacy, and forgive one's old vices.

（何艳 译）★●

9. Forgive others' small mistakes, forget long-standing enmities, and do not expose others' shameful secrets.

（冯雷 译）●●

10. Don't mock someone for their mistakes, don't share someone else's secrets, don't hold grudges.

（瑞雪 译）●●

11. Forgive other people's small faults, respect their privacy and forget their misdoings.

（曹小菁 译）●●

12. Forgive small faults; respect others' privacy; forget old grudges.

（石爱伟 译）★

13. It's inadvisable to reprove others for their slight mistakes, disclose others' private information or bear a grudge against others for their evil deeds in the past.

（王毅 译）★

【191】文章做到极处，无有他奇，只是恰好；人品做到极处，无有他异，只是本然。

——洪应明《菜根谭》

投票：外方评委3人投票★，中方评委3人投票●

1. The best writing is to the point. The best virtue is to be yourself.

（王如利 译）★★★●●●

2. The best writing is but the right expression; the best character is but to follow the nature.

（王成杰 译）●●●

3. An article well written has nothing unique but exactness; a character well cultivated has nothing different but naturalness.

（倪庆行 译）★●

4. Appropriateness is all for a good article and genuineness is all for a great character.

（冯雷 译）★●

5. For an article, being just right describes the superb art. For a person, the supreme state lies in following the heart.

（石永浩 译）●●

6. When an essay is natural, it's just right. When a person has good character, it's natural.

(陶家乐 译) ★

7. There's nothing special about a well-written article but appropriate style;
there's nothing special about an admirable character but natural grace.

(石爱伟 译) ★

8. To achieve one's best writing, one must be precise. To be one's best self,
one must return to their own nature.

(方必怡 译) ★

9. Good writing is achieved by nothing fancy but the harmony of all elements. Noble character is cultivated by nothing unusual but being honest
and natural.

(何艳 译) ★

【192】有意栽花花不发，无心插柳柳成荫。——《增广贤文》

投票：外方评委2人投票★，中方评委2人投票●

1. Flowers planted on purpose don't bloom, but willow twigs stuck casually
boom.

(魏红霞 译) ★●

2. Flowers grown deliberately bud not; willows planted inadvertently present
shade a lot.

(任诚刚 译) ●●

3. Carefully-planted flowers may fail to bud against our wish, while casual-
ly-placed willow twigs may flourish.

(张俊锋 译) ●●

4. Sometimes you reap not what you sow, but you unintentionally grow.

（杨秀波 译）●●

5. I carefully grow my flowers, but some just don't blow; I casually plant willow twigs, and they all lushly grow.

（冯雷 译）●●

6. It is sometimes unbelievable that the more you work hard on it, the more you fail easily, and the more you put it aside, the more you succeed easily.

（艾朝阳 译）★

7. Things don't always happen as planned. That's how we should life understand.

（王昌玲 译）★

8. Flower trees are planted in vain, and willow shade is casually gained.

（曹小菁 译）★

【193】 是非终日有，不听自然无。——《增广贤文》

投票：外方评委9人投票★，中方评委4人投票●

1. Gossip dies without an audience.

（马建军 译）★★★★★★★★●

2. Gossip ceases once you ignore it.

（王昌玲 译）★★★★★

3. There's gossip every day; turning a deaf ear is the best way.

（魏红霞 译）★●●●

4. Deaf to gossips, peaceful in mind.

（石永浩 译）★★●

5. Yes or no, out of your control; listen or not, your choice though.

（钱朝晖 译）★ ●

6. Rumors stop with the wise.

（刘向军 译）★ ●

7. Gossips cease running when people turn a deaf ear to them.

（吴春晓 译，投票后修改）● ●

8. Gossip is anywhere if you care and nowhere if you turn a deaf ear.

（王毅 译）● ●

9. Shut your ears and you will be free from all gossips and rumors.

（石爱伟 译）★

10. Gossip will die if no one trusts it.

（陶家乐 译）★

11. There are arguments. Stay away from them and you will find peace in the quietness.

（董庆瑗 译）★

【194】人不劝不善，钟不打不鸣。——《增广贤文》

投票：外方评委 9 人投票★，中方评委 5 人投票●

1. Men are taught to be good just as bells are struck to ring.

（王毅 译）★ ★ ★ ★ ★ ● ● ● ●

2. One needs to be educated to be well round, just like a bell needs to be rung to make a sound.

（孙玲玲 译）★ ★ ★ ★ ★ ● ●

3. People are taught to be good, not born with goodness; bells are struck to chime, not made with chimes.

（吴春晓 译）●●●

4. Man needs admonitions to be good, as a bell needs striking to peal.

（叶如钢 译）★●

5. Bells need knocks to ring, and men need advice to progress.

（冯雷 译）★●

6. Advise other people for them to keep their original mind; ring the bell for it to tell the scheduled time.

（曹小菁 译）★●

7. Men do more good deeds when encouraged, just as bells emit louder sound when rung with more effort.

（刘向军 译）★★

8. Exhortation melts a man, as striking rings a bell.

（王成杰 译）●●

9. Bell chimes when struck and humans progress when lectured.

（王梅兰 译）●●

10. An upright man must keep the warn of self-discipline, just like a bell sounds with strike.

（郁序新 译）★

11. Strikes can toll a bell or toughen a man.

（石永浩 译）★

【195】君子爱财，取之有道。——《增广贤文》

投票：外方评委8人投票★，中方评委4人投票●

1. It's human nature to yearn for wealth, but a nobleman acquires it righteously.

（孙玲玲 译）★★★●●●

2. Men of virtue obtain wealth by proper means.

（王毅 译）★★★★

3. Gentlemen acquire money by justified means.

（王绍昌 译）★★★★

4. Everybody likes money, but remember to get it legally.

（张莹 译）●●●

5. A gentleman earns money in an honest way.

（冯雷 译）★●

6. A noble man makes money in a proper way.

（董秀静 译）★★

7. A noble person gets riches from legal means and not from illegal ways.

（陶家乐 译）★

8. Noble men love money too, but they get it in righteous ways.

（王梅兰 译）★

9. A man of virtue only creates wealth through the proper channels rather than by illegal means.

（郁序新 译）★

【196】少年读书，如隙中窥月；中年读书，如庭中望月；老年读书，如台上玩月。

——张潮《幽梦影》

投票：外方评委8人投票★，中方评委7人投票●

1. Reading in youth is like peeping at the moon through a crevice; reading in one's prime is like gazing at the moon in the courtyard, while reading in old age is like appreciating the moon from a terrace. One's understanding deepens with age and experience.

（王昌玲 译）★★★★●●●●●

2. Reading books at young age is like peeping at the moon through the curtain; at middle age, looking up in the courtyard; at old age, enjoying it from the balcony.

（张晔 译）★★★★★★●

3. Reading feels somewhat like viewing the moon differently at distinct stages of life: young, peeping curiously through a crack; middle-aged, gazing musingly from a courtyard; old, enjoying leisurely on a balcony.

（石永浩 译）★●●●●●

4. Reading, for teenagers is like peeping at the moon through a crevice, for the mid-aged like watching it from a courtyard, and at the old age like enjoying it from a balcony.

（叶如钢 译）●●●●

5. Reading in youth is like peering the moon through a crevice; in middle age, like appreciating it in a yard; in old age, like having fun with it on a platform.

（杨秀波 译）●●●●

6. A book is like the moon. A young reader is curious about it; an adult reader understands it; an old reader enjoys it.

（冯雷 译）●●●

7. A book is like the moon. A kid just gets a glimpse, an adult finds it captivating and only a ripe old man discovers a companion.

（樊功生 译）★●

8. A book is like the moon. Kids take it as a picture to draw. Adults take it as a subject to learn. The aged take it as magic to show.

（郁序新 译）★●

【197】花不可以无蝶，山不可以无泉，石不可以无苔，水不可以无藻，乔木不可以无藤萝，人不可以无癖。

——张潮《幽梦影》

投票：外方评委8人投票★，中方评委9人投票●

1. Butterflies add romance to a flower; a spring gives elegance to a hill; moss bestows spirit upon a rock; algae imparts charm to a pond; vines increase holiness of a tree, hobbies make a person more interesting.

（冯雷 译）●●●●●●●●

2. A hovering butterfly gives a flower life; the gurgling stream makes the mountain alive; the green moss beautifies the rockery; the growing algae decorates the pond; the climbing ivy embraces the tree. A particular hobby makes an interesting person.

（石爱伟 译）★●●●●●

3. Flowers can't do without butterflies, mountains can't do without springs, rocks can't do without moss, water can't do without algae, trees can't do without vines, and people can't do without hobbies.

（王昌玲 译）★★★★★★

4. A flower kissed by a butterfly is more lovely, a mountain with a spring is more lively, a stone covered with moss is more charming, water with algae is more transparent, trees with vines are more forestlike, and a man with a favorite is more attractive.

（艾朝阳 译）★★●●●

5. Flowers aren't fragrant without butterflies; mountains aren't mysterious without fountains; rocks aren't mighty without mosses; waters aren't profound without algae; woods aren't luxuriant without vines; and men aren't complete without hobbies.

（杨中仁 译）★●●●

6. Butterflies sweeten flowers; springs moisten mountains; moss enlivens rocks; duckweeds embellish ponds; vines enshrine trees; interests endear men.

（石永浩 译）★●●●

7. Flowers cannot do without butterflies, nor can mountains without fountains, nor can stones without mosses, nor can waters without algae, nor can trees without vines and nor can men without hobbies.

（倪庆行 译）●●●

8. No flowers bloom without butterflies; no mountains spire without springs; no stones lie without mosses; no water reflects without algae; no trees grow without vines; no men live without hobbies.

（魏红霞 译）●●●

9. All lives adorn each other. Butterflies embellish flowers; springs enliven mountains; mosses decorate stones; algae grace waters; vines beautify trees while hobbies enhance humans.

（王绍昌 译）●●●

10. Dull are flowers without butterflies, a hill without fountains, a rock without moss, a lake without water grass, a tree without winding vines, and a man without something he indulges in.

（铁冰 译）●●●

【198】邦以民为本，民以食为天，财者食之原。

——吕熊《女仙外史》

投票：外方评委9人投票★，中方评委5人投票●

1. People are to a nation what food is to a person. One cannot get food without money, not to mention the prosperity of a nation.

（李慧 译）★★★★●

2. A country is based on its people, people are based on grain, and grain is based on wealth.

（华卫 译）★★★●

3. A state will not thrive if not supported by the people; the people cannot survive if not sustained by food supply; food supply may not suffice if not propped by economic prosperity.

（石永浩 译）★●●●

4. People are the very foundation of a nation, food is the first necessity of people and wealth is the prime source of food.

（史红霞 译）★●

5. Any country, basically relies on its civilians. Any civilian, essentially relies on food. Any food, ultimately relies on moneybag.

（张晓阳 译）★★

名言警句英译

6. Governance is people-oriented; bread is the staff of life; wealth ensures the supply of food.

（王成杰 译）●●

7. The prosperity of a state is dependent on its people whose livelihood rely on food which is purchased by hard-earned money. (So reduce taxation and the people will benefit and thrive; in turn the state will be strong.)

（石爱伟 译）●●

8. A country should see people as its foundation. Food is the people's living precondition. Fortune is the source of food.

（倪庆行 译）●●

9. People are of fundamental importance for a state; food is of paramount necessity for people; wealth is the primary source for food.

（王毅 译）●●

10. A nation rises from its root in people's interest, just as people take food as priority, so the good combination of government and people is the best source of a great country.

（郁序新 译）★

11. People are the foundation of a nation; food is a must for a person; so reducing taxes is a ruler's obligation.

（冯雷 译）★

【199】室雅何须大，花香不在多。——郑板桥 五言联

投票：外方评委5人投票★，中方评委5人投票●

1. Elegant rooms needn't be spacious; fragrant flowers needn't be numerous.

（石永浩 译1）★★★★●●●●●

2. A small room can excel in elegance, and a single flower can exude ample fragrance.

(叶如钢 译) ★ ★ ★ ★ ● ● ● ● ●

3. An elegant room is fine regardless of its size; a fragrant flower is sweet even it is single.

(刘群 译) ★ ★ ★ ★ ●

4. The size does not decide the elegance of a room; the cluster does not determine the fragrance of a bloom.

(乐国斌 译) ★ ★ ★ ●

5. The size of a room doesn't decide the elegance; the amount of flowers doesn't mean the fragrance.

(赵宜忠 译) ★ ● ● ●

6. The elegance of abodes lies not in the size; the fragrance of flowers rests not with the amount.

(石永浩 译2) ★ ● ●

7. A house in good taste is not necessarily spacious; flowers exuding aroma can be small in number.

(李红雨 译) ★ ★ ★

8. Size doesn't matter for a fine room; number, neither, for sweet roses.

(张俊锋 译) ★ ★ ★

9. Rooms, even if small, could be elegant; flowers, even if a few, could be fragrant.

(程永生 译) ● ● ●

10. Nice enough is a small exquisite room; sweet enough is a few flowers' perfume.

(铁冰 译) ● ● ●

11. An exquisite room is not necessarily large; a few fragrant flowers will suffice.

(倪庆行 译) ★ ●

12. Not spacious, my room is still filled with elegance; not in a myriad, flowers still give off fragrance.

（许霖越 译）★

13. It is not the size of space that produces elegance for a room; it is not the number of flowers that determines the density of fragrance.

（冯雷 译）★

【200】好便宜者，不可与之交财。多狐疑者，不可与之谋事。

——陈宏谋《五种遗规·训俗遗规·卷四》

投票：外方评委 12 人投票★，中方评委 10 人投票●

1. Don't get involved with people who are financially greedy and socially distrustful.

（王成杰 译）★★★★★★★★★★★★●●●

2. Do not involve yourself economically with those who covet petty advantages. Do not seek counsel from those who are suspicious.

（倪庆行 译）★★★★★●●●●

3. Don't partner financially with the avaricious; don't team up with the suspicious.

（石永浩 译1）★★★★★●●

4. Never develop business partnership with a mean profit seeker, nor build friendship with one who lives in suspicion.

（冯雷 译）★●●●●●

5. Never share wealth with those who love petty gains. Never cooperate with those who are very suspicious.

（张晓阳 译）●●●●●

6. The avaricious shouldn't be your business partners; the suspicious never make good teammates.

（石永浩 译2）●●●●●

7. Conduct no business with the greedy; cooperate not with the oversuspicious.

（王昌玲 译）★●●●

8. Don't have financial association with a greedy guy; and don't collaborate with a suspicious soul.

（杨中仁 译）●●●●

9. Neither have business with those fond of petty gain. Nor plan matters with those suffering suspicious pain.

（华卫 译）●●●

10. In financial matters avoid people who take advantage of others, in joint endeavors avoid people who do not trust others.

（叶如钢 译）★●

11. Never do business with those who are covetous; never negotiate with those who are suspicious.

（王勣 译）★●

12. Don't count on those who like taking advantages of other, neither bank on those who like doubting partners around them.

（郁序新 译）★●

【201】心病终须心药治，解铃还是系铃人。

——曹雪芹《红楼梦》第九十回

投票：外方评委9人投票★，中方评委7人投票●

1. Just as the best doctor for a mental problem is the person who caused it, the best person to take the bell off the tiger is one who tied it.

（冯雷 译）●●●●●●●

2. Problems are better solved by those who caused them.

（石爱伟 译）★★★★★

3. To solve a mental problem you must start from the mind；to disentangle a complicated knot you'd better find the knotter.

（石永浩 译1）●●●●●

4. A knot can only be unknotted by its knotter. A broken heart can only be warmed by its heart breaker.

（张晔 译）●●●●●

5. No remedy but love can cure the lovesick well；only the person who tied the knot can loosen the tiger's neck bell.

（倪庆行 译）★★●●

6. Mental maladies can only be cured by resorting to the mind；problems are best solved by turning to the trouble maker.

（王绍昌 译）★●

7. The best remedy for one's mental illness is his inner strength，whoever made the trouble should end it himself.

（张晓阳 译）★★

8. To remedy the mind you should find out the mental factor；to undo a knot you may turn to the knotter.

（石永浩 译2）●●

【202】月满则亏，水满则溢。——曹雪芹《红楼梦》第十三回

投票：外方评委 10 人投票★，中方评委 7 人投票●

1. A full moon wanes. A full glass of water spills. Things dwindle after their peaks.

（王梅兰 译）●●●●●●

2. All our lives wax and wane, just like the moon.

（刘向军 译）★★★★★

3. When reaching their limit, things begin to turn around.

（冯雷 译）★●●

4. Everything has its limitation.

（张莹 译）★★★

5. Things may backfire if they are overdone.

（杨中仁 译）★●

6. Once the moon becomes full it wanes, once water has filled it overflows; pushed to the limit, all things fall apart.

（杨胜悦 译）★★

7. The moon wanes when it gets full round; water overflows when a mug brims with it.

（郁序新 译）●●

8. When the moon waxes to its fullest, it will wane; when water rises to the brim, it will spill.

（倪庆行 译）●●

9. Aside waxes are wanes; atop prosperity is poverty.

（王绍昌 译）●●

10. The full and round moon wanes; the fully-filled cup overflows.

（石爱伟 译）●●

11. The moon will wane when it is full, the very mirror of our life.

（石永浩 译）★

12. When the moon is full, it will wane. When water is too much, it will overflow.

（马建军 译）★

13. A full moon tends to become a crescent, and a full cup of water tends to overflow.

（孙玲玲 译）★

14. The moon would wane the moment it becomes full, the cup would overflow when overfilled. Therefore, don't go to extremes in order to last long.

（王毅 译）★

【203】江山代有才人出，各领风骚数百年。

——赵翼《论诗五首·其二》

投票：外方评委3人投票★，中方评委5人投票●

1. Each generation has its talents bright, for a few centuries they stand at great height.

（叶如钢 译）★●●●●●

2. Talents of generations have surely come out here; each can lead cultural progress for many a myriad year.

（任诚刚 译）●●●●●

3. Talents emerge from each generation, and boast of hundreds of years' literary domination.

（倪庆行 译）★●●

4. The world has talented heroes for each generation to influence centuries.

（艾朝阳 译）★●

5. Nations bring out outstanding talents and their great ideas are inherited for generations.

（郁序新 译）★●

6. Each nation produces great talents for their generation; over the centuries their unrivaled works have led the literary fashion.

（冯雷 译）●●

7. Each generation sees talents come to prominence; people in later centuries still sense their influence.

（石永浩 译）●●

8. In the country for generations many talented people appear, their poetry and maxims have been passed down for so many a year.

（赵宜忠 译）★

9. Each generation, each century boasts its own gorgeous talents.

（铁冰 译）★

【204】苟利国家生死以，岂因祸福避趋之。

——林则徐《赴戍登程口占示家人》

投票：外方评委8人投票★，中方评委7人投票●

1. For better or for worse, I'm willing to die for the good of my country.

（杨中仁 译）★★★★★★●

2. I would rather die for the good of my country than think too much about my personal weal and woe.

（王成杰 译）★●●●●

3. For my nation, I don't care about personal gain or loss; when needed, I will sacrifice my life.

（冯雷 译）★★★★

4. I'd sacrifice my life for the benefit of the whole nation. How can fortune or misfortune ever change my dedication?

（王昌玲 译）★●●

5. For what benefit the country I can die, how would I shun them because my risks are high?

（叶如钢 译）●●●

6. As long as it is beneficial to my country, I would rather go through any dangers even if it means sacrificing my life.

（孙玲玲 译）●●●

7. Death is not a threat if what I do can benefit my country; personal gain or loss is no concern of mine.

（石爱伟 译）★●

8. I won't hesitate to sacrifice my life for the best of my country, never will I run away because of danger or my own safety.

（董庆瑗 译）★●

9. In the interest of my country, I'd jeopardize my life, let alone bear misfortunes.

（刘向军 译）●●

10. So long as my death serves my country well, I won't flinch from the tolling of my knell.

（吴春晓 译）●●

11. No matter what woes I encounter, I shall dedicate my life to my motherland.

（倪庆行 译）●●

12. To my country I know my life I owe; high and low I go, caring not my weal and woe.

（王绍昌 译）●●

13. As long as it is in the best interest of my motherland, even the risk of losing my life will not daunt me, let alone personal gains or losses.

（石永浩 译）●●

14. For the interest of my nation, I am ready to sacrifice anything, weighing not personal losses or gains.

（王毅 译）★

15. I would make a sacrifice for the benefits of my country; how could I fend it off because of my personal adversity.

（王梅兰 译）★

16. I will dedicate my whole life to serve my country regardless of fortune or misfortune.

（张立国 译）★

【205】海到无边天作岸，山登绝顶我为峰。

——林则徐《出老》

投票：外方评委9人投票★，中方评委5人投票●

1. The skyline anchors the boundless water; the conqueror dwarfs the towering mountain.

（王成杰 译）★★★●●

2. The sea stretches far to meet the sky; a man stands atop to be the peak high.

（马建军 译）●●●●

3. At the end of the sea, the skyline is the coastline; on the top of the mountain, I am the peak.

（张晓阳 译）★●●

4. The sea is boundless as far as the horizon, and the mountain is infinite as high as I can reach.

（邢珽 译）★★★

5. The azure sky drapes the blue sea; the high peak is now crested by me.

（石永浩 译）★★★

6. Stretching far beyond sight, the boundless sea merges into one with the distant sky; standing atop the majestic mountain, I'm the peak of the peak towering high.

（王毅 译）●●●

7. The sky is the shore of the sea when it reaches its end, I'm the peak of the mountain when I stand at its top.

（杨中仁 译）★●

8. Afar, the skyline defines the vast sea; atop the peak, I feel at my acme.

（吴春晓 译）★●

9. Boundless, the sea's shore is the sky; on the mountain top, I am the peak.

（叶如钢 译）★★

10. A skyline is the end of a sea. A summitting climber is the mountain peak.

（王梅兰 译）●●

11. The sea ends in a shore, and the shore is the sky; the mountain culminates in a crest, and the crest is me.

（田璐 译）★

【206】 落红不是无情物，化作春泥更护花。

——龚自珍《己亥杂诗·其五》

投票：外方评委4人投票★，中方评委8人投票●

1. Red fallen flowers are no heartless being; they melt into mud to nourish more buds next spring.

（张俊锋 译）★●●●●●●

2. A fallen petal still has love and heart, in nourishing flowers it plays a part.

（冯雷 译1）★★●●●●●

3. The fallen petals red are not a heartless thing—they'll melt in the earth to nourish the blooming spring.

（铁冰 译）●●●●

4. Fallen flowers are not objects without heart; into spring mud, to spring flowers, they become a part.

（王绍昌 译1）★★●

5. Flowers fade to the earth to breed more.

（艾朝阳 译）★★●

6. Flower petals wither and dry and fall, they're dead in body but not for love at all; they turn themselves into the spring soil, to nurture the new buds with gardeners' toil.

（冯雷 译2）★★

7. Falling flowers are not things of no heart; turning into soil, they'll nourish spring buds.

（王昌玲 译）●●

8. It isn't heartless for flowers to fall; in spring soil, they're helpful to more.

（魏红霞 译）●●

9. Heartless are not fallen petals, in soil they nurture spring flowers.

（叶如钢 译）●●

10. The fallen flowers are nothing heartless, but after turning into spring mud, they'll also provide nutrients for later flowers.

（赵宜忠 译）★

11. Fallen petals are not ruthless themselves. They turn into spring mud at all hours to nurture and nourish new flowers.

（王绍昌 译2）★

【207】我劝天公重抖擞，不拘一格降人才。

——龚自珍《己亥杂诗·其二百二十》

投票：外方评委4人投票★，中方评委5人投票●

1. Heaven, I pray that you rejuvenate, and myriads of talents initiate.

（王绍昌 译1）●●●●●

2. Heaven, please renew your vitality and splendor, and render, to the world, talents of all walks of life.

（王绍昌 译2）★★★●

3. Oh Heaven, could you become invigorated once more, and bless our long-benighted country with talents galore?

（铁冰 译）★●●●

4. May Heaven its grandeur extend, and let all talents to Earth descend.

（叶如钢 译1）●●●●

5. Hurrah, God! With thy powerful rejuvenation, may the world be blessed with stars of innovation!

（樊功生 译）★★●

6. Oh, Heaven, shall I pray thee to re-shake, and rain talents, whatever it may take?

（王昌玲 译）●●●

7. I pray thee, Lord, steep in splendor again, and bless us with various talented men.

（刘群 译）★

8. I will plead with the imperial court not to be yoked when selecting talents.

（倪庆行 译）●

9. Heaven, bring out thy vigor again, and on Earth all kinds of talents rain.

（叶如钢 译2）●

10. Heaven shakes, and stars fall. Thanks Heaven, and welcome stars!

（艾朝阳 译）●

11. Heaven, would you please string up your nerves? We'll share various talent reserves.

（魏红霞 译）●

【208】履不必同，期于适足；治不必同，期于利民。

——魏源《默觚下·治篇五》

投票：外方评委6人投票★，中方评委4人投票●

1. Good shoes fit your feet; good governments benefit the people.

（张俊锋 译）★★★★●

2. Shoes that fit are good shoes; governance that brings benefits to people is good governance.

（冯雷 译）★★●●●

3. Good shoes fit the feet; good governance benefits the people.

（石爱伟、王成杰 译）★★●●

4. Shoes can vary as long as they fit one's feet; governance of a country can differ as long as it benefits people.

（何艳 译）★★●

5. It's unreasonable for the people to wear the same shoes, they should find what suit their feet; nor is it reasonable for the governments to adopt the same model of governance, they should find what benefits their people.

（张晓阳 译）★★★

6. Shoes don't have to be the same for the sake of feet; governance doesn't have to be the same for the sake of people.

（乐国斌 译）●●●

7. Like different shoes for different feet, different governances suit different countries.

（王梅兰 译）★●

8. Shoes can be any styles as long as they fit. The way of governing can vary as long as it benefits the citizens.

（樊功生 译）★●

9. As people wear shoes that fit well, countries should be governed in different ways that are best for their people.

（马建军 译）★

10. Everyone's shoes don't have to be the same size, the key is to fit their feet; it is not necessary for every country to adopt the same governance method. What is important is to benefit the country and the people.

（任诚刚 译）★

11. It's unnecessary for shoes and models of governance to be identical; different shoes suit different feet; different models of governance are for different people.

（曹小菁 译）★

12. Just as the best pair of shoes suits your feet, the best method of administration benefits the people.

(王昌玲 译) ★

【209】成大事者，以识为主，以才为辅。

——曾国藩《曾国藩家书》

投票：外方评委6人投票★，中方评委3人投票●

1. Vision often takes precedence over capability for great achievers.

(石爱伟 译) ★★★●●●

2. Talent gives way to vision when it comes to making one great.

(丁如伟 译) ★★★●

3. Talent helps one achieve; vision helps one achieve big.

(冯雷 译) ★●●

4. A great achiever depends mainly on his insight, and then his talent.

(王成杰 译) ●●●

5. Outstanding people are more known for foresight and insight than talents and abilities.

(王绍昌 译) ●●

6. To achieve something important, broaden your perspective and sharpen your skills.

(陶家乐 译) ●●

7. To have great achievements, knowledge and planning come first and then action.

(艾朝阳 译) ★

名言警句英译

8. To achieve great feats, we should resort mainly to our incisive perspicacity, in addition to being supplemented by talents.

（倪庆行 译）★

9. Perspicacity complemented by capacity ensures your success.

（叶步青 译）★

【210】 利可共而不可独，谋可寡而不可众。

——曾国藩《六戒》

投票：外方评委6人投票★，中方评委4人投票●

1. Benefits should be shared by all, yet decision making should involve fewer people.

（马建军 译）★★★★

2. Profit must be shared; stratagems must be secret.

（乐国斌 译）★★●

3. Benefits must not be monopolized while strategies must not be publicized.

（倪庆行 译）★★★

4. A profit is to be shared; a plot is to be self-cared.

（崔传明 译）●●●

5. Share benefits, but hide schemes.

（王成杰 译）★●

6. Gains must be shared; schemes must be kept secret.

（叶如钢 译）★●

7. Though profit must be shared, schemes must be kept to oneself.

(杨胜悦 译) ★ ●

8. Benefits shall not be monopolied; tactics and strategies shall not be shared by many.

(张俊锋 译) ★ ●

9. While benefits must be shared, a scheme must be worked out alone.

(何艳 译) ★ ●

10. Profits should be shared among people and strategies should be kept in secrets.

(孙玲玲 译) ★ ●

11. Benefits should be shared by all; while decisions should be made among a few.

(张晓阳 译) ★ ●

12. Share benefits together rather than privately; make strategies confidentially rather than openly.

(郁序新 译) ★ ★

13. Profit should be shared; plot should not be revealed.

(任诚刚 译) ● ●

14. Benefits should be shared, plans should not.

(瑞雪 译) ★

15. Profits are better to be shared to as many people as possible; too many proposals often spoil a plan.

(石爱伟 译) ★

名言警句英译

【211】以廉律己，以勤治事，以公处人。

——曾国藩，收录于《曾文正公学案》

投票：外方评委7人投票★，中方评委3人投票●

1. Discipline yourself with integrity, govern affairs with diligence, and treat others with justice.

（曹小菁 译）★★★●

2. Discipline yourself to be honest and clean, perform your duties with diligence, and treat others with justice.

（马建军 译）★●●●

3. Uphold integrity, work with diligence, and treat others with fairness.

（王梅兰 译）★★★★

4. There are three life principles: disciplining myself with integrity; doing jobs with diligence; treating others with justice.

（陈丽珠 译）★●●

5. Discipline yourself with integrity, perform duties with diligence, and treat others with justice.

（丁如伟 译）★●●

6. Discipline yourself with purity, handle affairs with diligence, and treat people with justice.

（倪庆行 译）★★★

7. Discipline oneself, work diligently, and treat people fairly.

（田璐 译）★★★

8. Be self-disciplined, hardworking and fair-minded.

（王如利 译）★★★

9. As an official, one should be just, dutiful and uncorrupted.

（石永浩 译）★●

10. Live simply, work hard and be fair.

（吴春晓 译）★★

11. Be self-disciplined, be diligent, and be fair.

（何艳 译）★★

12. Be a man with clean hands, diligent in performing duties and impartial in dealing with people.

（王毅 译）●●

13. A civil servant must discipline himself against corruption, be diligent in his work, and protect public interests in dealing with people.

（石爱伟 译）★

14. Discipline self with decency; conduct business with diligence; engage others with fairness.

（王绍昌 译）★

15. Government officials should be honest, self-disciplined, diligent and treat everybody fairly.

（董秀静 译）★

【212】物来顺应，未来不迎。当时不杂，既过不恋。

——曾国藩　收录于《曾胡治兵语录》

投票：外方评委4人投票★，中方评委3人投票●

1. Don't worry about the future, don't dwell on the past, seize the day and let nature take its course.

（王成杰 译）★★●●●

2. Adapt to situations when they occur, and worry not about things which aren't yet there. Focus on one thing at a time, and let bygones be bygones.

（叶如钢 译）★ ●

3. Let nature take its course without interference. Live for the moment, not for the past.

（王如利 译）★ ★

4. Let go of the past and stop daydreaming; take whatever comes and stay focused.

（冯雷 译）★ ★

5. Be open and adaptable to whatever occurs in the future; live in the moment and don't cling to the past.

（王昌玲 译）★

6. Take a positive attitude to what happened or what will happen, and concentrate on what you do now and what you will do in the future.

（郁序新 译）★

7. How should we live our lives? Face the challenge when it comes; no need to worry about the future; concentrate on one thing at a time; never revel in the past.

（张晔 译）★

8. Adapt to the changes of the world, believe in your future. Focus on what's right in front of you, and let bygones be bygones.

（张晓阳 译）★

9. We should take things as they come, live and keep calm in the moment. We shouldn't worry too much about the future or cling to the past.

（董秀静 译）★

【213】 能受天磨真铁汉，不遭人嫉是庸才。

——左宗棠《无题》

投票：外方评委9人投票★，中方评委5人投票●

1. Adversity reveals a man；envy tells a genius.

（吴春晓 译）★ ★ ★ ★ ● ●

2. A true grit comes from adversities，only mediocrity can avoid jealousies.

（樊功生 译）★ ● ●

3. He who survives torture is really something. He who is never envied is actually nothing.

（董庆瑗 译）● ● ●

4. The tough can stand the test of any ordeal，the mediocre get envied by none at all.

（王昌玲 译）★ ●

5. A true man survives from difficulty；a mean man frees from jealousy.

（崔传明 译）★ ●

6. Don't fear trials，because they make you strong；don't let others' green envy bother you，because it's proof that you're outstanding.

（石爱伟 译）★ ●

7. Adversity makes a genius，to be envied by others.

（马建军 译）★ ●

8. Ordeals forge enviable talent.

（刘向军 译）★

【214】日日行，不怕千万里；常常做，不怕千万事。

——金缨《格言联璧·处事类》

投票：外方评委9人投票★，中方评委7人投票●

1. Ten thousand miles won't be far if you keep walking day by day; ten thousand tasks won't be hard if you keep doing them piece by piece.

（冯雷 译）★★★★★★●●●●

2. Journeys are made, step by step; missions are accomplished, bit by bit.

（王绍昌 译）●●●●●●●

3. An inch a day, you will cover the longest journey; one thing a day, you will accomplish a lot.

（王昌玲 译1）★★★●●

4. However long and arduous a journey is, just foot it day by day; however tough and complex a mission is, just tackle it bit by bit.

（石永浩 译）★●●●●●

5. Daily persistence leads to thousands of accomplishments.

（樊功生 译）★★★●

6. Walk on day after day and you won't fear long trek at all. Often do and you won't fear anything big or small.

（赵宜忠 译）●●●●

7. A step a day makes a journey of a thousand miles. A bit a day will dismantle a skyscraper of a million bricks.

（艾朝阳 译）★●●

8. Keeping walk every day shortens thousands of miles, keeping work very often lessens thousands of trifles.

（郁序新 译1）●●●

9. A journey of thousands of miles is nothing to a man walking daily; if one does things time and again, he'll achieve great things then.

（魏红霞 译）★ ●

10. Bit by bit, persistence succeeds.

（王昌玲 译2）★ ★

11. Keeping walk day by day leads a good way to peak. Keeping work step by step makes hard stuff meek.

（郁序新 译2）● ●

【215】知足常足，终身不辱；知止常止，终身不耻。

——金缨《格言联璧·惠吉类》

投票：外方评委5人投票★，中方评委5人投票●

1. Contentment and self-discipline spare one from disgrace.

（王昌玲 译）★ ★ ● ● ●

2. Self-contentment invites no shame; self-moderation incurs no blame.

（崔传明 译）★ ● ● ● ●

3. A man who is contented feels no shame; a man who knows when to stop incurs no blame.

（马建军 译）★ ● ●

4. Contented, you won't be disgraced; restrained, you won't be dishonoured.

（王梅兰 译）● ●

5. Very little is needed to make a happy life; it is all within yourself, in your way of thinking. Keep good attitude to all and you will be self-satisfied.

（郁序新 译）★ ★

6. To make your life honorable, be content and restrained.

（刘向军 译）●●

7. A simple life won't make you lose face; a greedy heart will bring you disgrace.

（冯雷 译）●●

8. Be wise to know when to press on and when to stop, and you'll neither humiliate others nor feel humiliated.

（吴春晓 译）★

9. Being contented and moderate keeps one dignified.

（石永浩 译）★

10. If we count our blessings and do things in a measured manner, we'll never be disgraced by greed or misbehavior.

（王成杰 译）★

[216] 事不可做尽，言不可道尽，势不可倚尽，福不可享尽。

——金缨《格言联璧·持躬类》

投票：外方评委6人投票★，中方评委3人投票●

1. Always be moderate in words and deeds. Never go too far in privilege or pleasures.

（石永浩 译）★★★★●●●

2. Never go to extremes in speaking or acting, nor exhaust your resources or good fortune.

（马建军 译）★★●●

3. Whatever we say and do, we should leave room and allow for unpredictable circumstances and needs.

（董秀静 译）★ ★ ●

4. We should avoid all extremes in what we do or say.

（乐国斌 译）★ ★ ★

5. Be moderate with your actions and words, power and luck.

（曹小菁 译）★ ●

6. No matter what you do, don't go to extremes.

（何冰 译）★ ●

7. Always leave room for other possibilities when you say or do something. Always save some for future use when you are gifted with power or fortune.

（王梅兰 译）● ●

8. Not everything should be done, not every word should be said, not all powers should be relied upon, and not all pleasures should be experienced.

（叶如钢 译）★

9. Matters should not be accomplished fully, words should not be stated fully, powers should not be utilized fully, and blessings should not be enjoyed fully.

（王绍昌 译）★

第五篇
近现代时期

Chapter V
Modern Period

【217】 不谋全局者，不足谋一域。

——陈澹然《寤言二·迁都建藩议》

投票：外方评委9人投票★，中方评委11人投票●

1. A good player plans across the board, a poor player moves an individual piece.

（冯雷 译1） ★★★★★★★★●●●●●●

2. Only one with global mindset can govern the region well.

（王绍昌 译1） ★★●●●●

3. Without an overall picture in mind, you cannot make a step.

（程永生 译1） ★★●●

4. He who cannot scheme the whole cannot scheme regionally.

（任诚刚 译） ●●●●

5. Only a holistic planner can be a great regional manager.

（王绍昌 译2） ★●●

6. Consideration of the whole situation preconditions a sound solution.

（冯雷 译2） ●●●

7. Those who do not take a global look cannot succeed in a local domain.

（张琼 译） ★●

8. If you can't see the whole, you can't do a part well at all.

（孟朝岗 译） ★●

9. Only the long-range perspective pans out well.

（王昌玲 译） ●●

10. Without the strategy in vision, one cannot develop effective tactics.

（程永生 译2） ●●

11. He can't govern regions small if he can't think overall.

（李红雨 译） ●●

12. Seek whole and you'll see partial.

（艾朝阳 译1）●●

13. You cannot see its speckles without seeing the egg.

（艾朝阳 译2）●●

【218】教育者，非为已往，非为现在，而专为将来。

——蔡元培

投票：外方评委6人投票★，中方评委3人投票●

1. Education is not for the past or the present, but for the future.

（杨秀波 译）★★★★●●

2. Rather than for the past or present, education is for the future.

（叶如钢 译）★●

3. Education is not for the past, nor for the present, but for the future.

（张晓阳 译）★●

4. Education serves neither the past nor the present, but the future.

（马百亮 译）★★

5. The purpose of education is not to change the past or the present, but to improve the future.

（刘德江 译）★★

6. The aim of education is not to reflect on the past, or to serve the present, but only to prepare for the future.

（马建军 译）●●

7. Neither for the past nor for the present, education aims at the future.

（王绍昌 译）●●

8. The purpose of education serves for the future of a nation rather than its past or its present.

(石爱伟 译) ★

9. Education is meant not for the past or the present, but solely for the future.

(张建惠 译) ★

10. Education is neither for the past nor for the present, but especially for the future.

(倪庆行 译) ★

11. Ultimately, education is intended for the future rather than the past or the present.

(石永浩 译) ★

12. Education is not for the benefit of the past and present, but for the benefit of the future.

(张立国 译) ★

13. Educators do not work for the past or the present but only for the future.

(董秀静 译) ★

【219】 水激石则鸣，人激志则宏。——秋瑾

投票：外方评委8人投票★，中方评委3人投票●

1. Strong willpower comes from constant exertion.

(叶步青 译) ★★★★●

2. If water hits the rock, it will roar. If a man gets motivated, he will soar.

（张莹 译）★●●

3. The water makes a loud sound when it strikes a rock. A person will aim high once the ambition is stirred.

（何艳 译）★★★

4. As a stone rumbles when getting beaten by water, a man will aim high when getting inspired.

（张晓阳 译）★●

5. Man is inspired to aspire, just as stones are water-swept to chime.

（王昌玲 译）★●

6. Rolling waves against rocks would roar; inspired men by others would soar.

（王毅 译）★●

7. The wave roars up high against rocks; so should a man set his aims high against setbacks.

（杨中仁 译）★●

8. Torrents send a stone resounding; challenges make a man aspiring.

（刘向军 译）●●

9. A torrent splashes when impeded by rocks; a man's will is the firmer when challenged.

（石爱伟 译）★

10. As water striking the rocks makes loud sounds, a man who is highly motivated aims high.

（马建军 译）★

11. Water pounds stones and stones sing. People aspire to be great, and people spring.

（孙玲玲 译）★

【220】 最是人间留不住，朱颜辞镜花辞树。

——王国维《蝶恋花·阅尽天涯离别苦》

投票：外方评委7人投票★，中方评委4人投票●

1. There's no such thing as forever; beauty fades and blossoms fall.

（马建军 译）★★★●

2. A thing of beauty will eventually fade, be it a fair flower or a flowery face.

（何冰 译）★★★★

3. O the greatest pity in the world; rosy cheeks fade in the mirror, fair blossoms fall off the tree.

（张俊锋 译）★★●

4. What are the most difficult things to remain in the world? O rosy faces in the mirrors and flying flowers in the wind.

（张晓阳 译）●●●

5. What men hold dearest, nature does recall—as all rosy cheeks fade in the mirrors, and flowers sadly bid their boughs farewell.

（吴春晓 译）★●

6. We cannot hold the time just as young faces in the mirror will become old and leaves will fall down from the tree one day.

（董秀静 译）★●

7. The most unavoidable farewells are when an aging face looked into the mirror and when a falling flower left the twig.

（田璐 译）●●

8. The falling flowers and one's youth will inevitably slip from our grasp.

（陶家乐 译）★

9. Unable to linger on, beauty withers along with flowers.

（樊功生 译）★

10. Alas! What are most unretainable in this world are the youthful look from the face and the blooming flowers from the trees.

（王毅 译）★

【221】横眉冷对千夫指，俯首甘为孺子牛。——鲁迅《自嘲》

投票：外方评委8人投票★，中方评委9人投票●

1. We never give way to our enemy, but we serve our people wholeheartedly.

（魏红霞 译）★★★★★★★★●●

2. Wild-eyed, I defy all the scoldings from the enemies. Head bowed, I serve my people like a willing horse.

（王成杰 译）★★●●●●●●●

3. Confront enemies' criticisms coldly, work for people wholeheartedly.

（杨秀波 译）★★★●●●

4. To the enemies, I am a fearless fighter coldly challenging their attack; for the people, I am a humble ox willing to carry them on my back.

（冯雷 译）●●●●●●

5. Furious browed, I glare at the common foe; head bowed, I stand as a willing ox for the people.

（张晓阳 译）★●●●●●

6. Eyebrow raised, I adamantly defy a thousand pointing fingers; head bowed, I willingly serve the people wholeheartedly like an ox.

（王绍昌 译）●●●●●

7. To reactionaries, I dare to defy their curse; for the people, I'd like to be a willing horse.

（杨中仁 译） ●●●●●

8. Venomous slander and numerous attacks with a stone face I fight back, but for the people and their righteous cause I'd bend my back and serve like a horse.

（石爱伟 译） ●●

9. To you foes' countless attack and assault, I shall unswervingly defy and no way surrender; to my people's need and demand, I shall willingly serve like a cow heart and soul.

（史红霞 译） ●●

10. Face contorted with rage, I defy the reactionaries frostily; head bowed with a will, I serve the demos heartily.

（丁如伟 译） ●●

11. Defiant when rebuked by foes, submissive when serving the folk.

（段永州 译） ★

【222】求利当求国民利，求名当求身后名。——马寅初

投票：外方评委3人投票★，中方评委4人投票●

1. Seek the benefits that benefit the nation and its people and the fame that long lives after my death.

（王毅 译） ★★●●●

2. Seek benefits for the people only, and achieve posthumous fame if any.

（叶如钢 译1） ★●●●

3. Seek fortune and fame that go with the interests of our people and country.

（吴春晓 译）★★

4. One who gives his nation a good name naturally gains his own lasting fame.

（石永浩 译）★★

5. Put the national interests above all and leave the personal fame behind death.

（郁序新 译）●●

6. The benefits I pursue are only for the people; the fame I aspire to is but posthumous.

（叶如钢 译2）★

7. We should seek for the well being of the people and the country as well as a good reputation of eternity.

（王昌玲 译）★

8. It's the benefit of the country one should strive for; it's fame after death one should seek.

（何艳 译）★

【223】所谓大学者，非谓有大楼之谓也，有大师之谓也。

——梅贻琦

投票：外方评委9人投票★，中方评委6人投票●

1. The glory of a university rests upon its great teachers and scholars rather than grand buildings.

（马建军 译）★★★★★●●

2. Great buildings don't make a university, but great scholars do.

(吴春晓 译) ★★●●●●

3. A university excels due to its scholars, not its buildings.

(史红霞 译) ★★★★★★

4. It is the greatness of its scholars, not the greatness of its buildings, that makes the greatness of a university.

(王成杰 译) ★★●●●

5. What makes a great university is not grand mansions but great masters.

(王昌玲 译) ★★●●●

6. The greatness of a university lies not in the magnificence of its buildings but in the excellence of its scholars.

(王毅 译) ★★●

7. It's the master scholars rather than magnificent buildings that make a great university.

(丁如伟 译) ★●●

8. The so-called university is backboned by the great scholars, not great buildings.

(张立国 译) ★●●

9. What defines a university is not great buildings but great minds.

(田璐 译) ★●●

10. A university is valued for its grand masters, not its grand buildings.

(董庆瑗 译) ★★★

11. It is not grand buildings but great scholars that make a university great.

(石永浩 译) ★●

12. A great university is not made by having great buildings, but great scholars.

(叶如钢 译) ★★

13. When it comes to university, it's glorious not for the graceful buildings, but for the great masters in it.

（杨中仁 译）★

14. Universities aren't the place where buildings stand but the place where talents stand out.

（魏红霞 译）★

15. A top university is famous for its top scholars, not tall buildings.

（冯雷 译）★

【224】做学问要在不疑处有疑，待人要在有疑处不疑。

——胡适

投票：外方评委6人投票★，中方评委3人投票●

1. Doubt is essential in an academic and scientific life but trust is important when dealing with people.

（石爱伟 译）★★★★●●

2. Be skeptical in learning, but treat others with trust.

（马建军 译）★●●●

3. Be questioning in learning and be trustful in life.

（王成杰 译）★★●

4. Be critical in pursuing knowledge and broad-minded in treating people.

（王毅 译）★★●

5. Be suspicious when learning, be trusting when talking to people.

（瑞雪 译）★★★

6. Do learning with a suspecting eye even when there is nothing to doubt; treat people with an unsuspecting heart even when there is something to doubt.

(丁如伟 译) ★ ●

7. In learning, doubt where there are no doubts; in human relations, avoid doubting where there are doubts.

(王绍昌 译) ★ ●

8. Be skeptical about your learning, but not about your friends.

(杨中仁 译) ★ ★

9. In studies and research, raise doubts where no doubt has been raised; when treating people, harbor no doubt where doubts are harbored by others.

(叶如钢 译) ● ●

10. Always be critical when doing research and the opposite when dealing with people.

(田璐 译) ● ●

11. In learning, question the seemingly unquestionable; in dealing with others, trust them in the shadow of distrust.

(张俊锋 译) ● ●

12. Doubt academically in the field of certainty. Give people the benefit of doubt.

(王昌玲 译) ★

【225】 板凳需坐十年冷，文章不写一句空。——韩儒林

投票：外方评委6人投票★，中方评委3人投票●

1. A true scholar persists in solid research with sincerity.

（王梅兰 译）★★★★

2. Perseverance and diligence lead to academic brilliance.

（王绍昌 译）★★★★

3. Better to be unknown to fame for a decade than to be renowned for reams of rubbish.

（丁如伟 译）★●

4. Good to be a bench warmer for ten years, but not to be a writer for empty words.

（杨中仁 译）●●

5. Rather than make up an article with one word in vain, I would sit on a back seat for ten years in pain.

（崔传明 译）●●

6. When you study, be focused and resilient; when you write, be brief and accurate.

（冯雷 译）★

7. As a scholar, one needs to focus on his studies, and write papers as a result of real constant studies.

（王婷 译）★

8. A true scholar can endure long periods of loneliness and his works can stand the test.

（王成杰 译）●

9. Ten years behind a desk is a necessary preparation for academic success; a well-written essay expresses substantial thoughts rather than show off flowery language.

（石爱伟 译）●

10. Sitting cold bench for ten years to endure loneliness to do research, I compile my paper without any empty talks.

（张立国 译）●

11. Better to sit on the cold bench for ten years than write anything trite.

（魏红霞 译）●

12. To take in, one need sit on a cold bench for ten years for education. To put out, one cannot bear half an empty word in composition.

（倪庆行 译）●

13. A great essay, needs years' dedication.

（董庆瑗 译）●

【226】一时强弱在于力，千秋胜负在于理。——曹禺

投票：外方评委7人投票★，中方评委3人投票●

1. Power may only win for the short term, but justice will prevail in the long run.

（张晓阳 译）★★★●●

2. Those with power are strong for a short while, whereas those in the right are victors in the long term.

（叶如钢 译）★★●●

3. Triumph by force will soon be past; victory of the truth will forever last.

（石永浩 译）★★●●

4. While temporary victory lies in the use of force, lasting victory consists in holding to the truth.

（何艳 译）★★●

5. Force may give you a temporary advantage, but reason determines the final outcome.

（王昌玲 译）★●●

6. While strength may gain the upper hand once in a while, justice will have a final say in the long run.

（王毅 译）★●

7. Power may dominate the moment, but reason will prevail forever.

（樊功生 译）★●

8. Force may prevail in a battle, but justice will win the war.

（王成杰 译）★★

9. Temporary victory is by strength, while eternal win is by upright truth.

（郁序新 译1）★★

10. Victory obtained by force is only temporary, while victory obtained with truth is timeless.

（董秀静 译）★★

11. Temporary strength is decided by might, while eternal victory is decided by right.

（倪庆行 译）●●

12. Having might wins the battle, but being right wins the war.

（吴春晓 译）★

13. One-time victory consists in strength; all-time victory, truth.

（乐国斌 译）★

14. The power of force will gradually weaken, and the victory of integrity and truth will last forever.

（郁序新 译2）★

【227】 勤能补拙是良训，一分辛劳一分才。——华罗庚

投票：外方评委8人投票★，中方评委4人投票●

1. Industry makes up where ingenuity lacks, for an ounce of sweat is worth an ounce of talent.

（叶步青 译）★ ★ ★ ★ ★

2. Diligence can make up for the inadequacy of talent.

（王昌玲 译）★ ★ ★ ★ ★

3. It is a truth generally acknowledged that diligence assists intelligence, and pains bring gains.

（石永浩 译）★ ● ● ●

4. Diligence is the cure for stupidity; talent is forged by toil and sweat.

（王毅 译）● ● ●

5. Practice is a cure for the non-gifted; one effort made is one gift re-granted.

（吴春晓 译）● ●

6. A good advice says that intelligence comes from diligence, so your sweat and toil will add you more talents.

（杨中仁 译）● ●

7. Hardworking redeems dullness; pains bring gains.

（王成杰 译）● ●

8. As a golden rule, diligence remedies one's dullness. Every assiduity contributes to your aptitude.

（刘群 译）● ●

9. Diligence amends deficiencies piece by piece; industry enhances capabilities bit by bit.

（冯雷 译）● ●

10. Work hard to achieve your goals.

（陶家乐 译）★

11. Hard work makes up for lack in other assets, a lifetime of toil will lead you to riches.

（杨胜悦 译）★

【228】人有三个基本错误是不能犯的：一是德薄而位尊，二是智小而谋大，三是力小而任重。

——南怀瑾

投票：外方评委6人投票★，中方评委3人投票●

1. People shouldn't make three basic mistakes: having a high position but little virtue; having a great ambition but little wisdom; having a heavy burden but little strength.

（董秀静 译）★★★★★●

2. People must not commit three basic mistakes: to occupy a respectable position with little virtue, to scheme big with scanty wisdom and to shoulder a weighty responsibility with feeble strength.

（倪庆行 译）★●●●

3. Three common mistakes for people to avoid: to have a little virtue but a high position, to have petty wisdom but a big plan, and to have puny strength but a heavy responsibility.

（王成杰 译）★●

4. There are three basic mistakes one should never make: being in a high position but not rich in virtue, making big plans but lacking wisdom, and taking great responsibility but lacking power.

（马建军 译）★●

5. A man must not commit the following three mistakes: a) occupying an important position without enough virtue; b) aspiring for too high an ambition without enough intellect; c) shouldering a heavy responsibility without enough ability.

(石爱伟 译) ★ ●

6. One should avoid three pitfalls in life, namely, being incompassionate but holding high office, unwise but pursuing grand goals, and incompetent but running great missions.

(吴春晓 译) ★ ★

7. Three basic mistakes should be avoided: thin virtue with a high position, tiny wisdom with a big plan, and little strength with a heavy responsibility.

(冯雷 译) ★ ★

8. If a man is degenerate while occupying a high position, incompetent while harbouring an overweening ambition, weak while carrying a heavy load, then he already commits three fundamental mistakes, which should be avoided by all.

(王毅 译) ★

9. There are three basic mistakes people should not make: one is that the low virtue is entrusted with a high position; the other is that the small wisdom is given a big stratagem to scheme; the third is that the weak capability is endowed with a heavy duty.

(任诚刚 译) ★

10. One should avoid three elementary mistakes: honor without morality, ambition without wisdom, and commitment without capability.

(乐国斌 译) ★

【229】重剑无锋，大巧不工。——金庸《神雕侠侣》

投票：外方评委7人投票★，中方评委3人投票●

1. A great sword needs no sharp edge；a great skill needs no subtlety.

（乐国斌 译）★ ★ ★ ★ ★ ● ●

2. A heavy sword needs no sharp blade；a great prowess is above and beyond small details.

（叶如钢 译）★ ★ ●

3. Great swordsmanship depends on skills rather than a sharp sword；great art depends on the artist's artistic vision rather than mere technique.

（石爱伟 译）★ ●

4. It's not the sword that wins fights but rather the one that wields the sword.

（陶家乐 译）★ ★

5. The use of a sword is not in its build but its wielder.

（杨胜悦 译）★ ★

6. Just as a heavy sword may not look sharp，true ingenuity is simple.

（王成杰 译）●

7. True swordplay does not depend on the blade；the really clever stuff is not so much about shape and detail as it should be.

（任诚刚 译）●

8. A powerful sword needs no sharp edge；a superb art reveals no skills of the artist.

（冯雷 译）●

9. A heavy sword needs no glaring blade；a superb art shows no striking craftsmanship.

（石永浩 译）●

【230】 愿你出走半生，归来仍是少年。

——孙衍《愿你出走半生，归来仍是少年》

投票：外方评委5人投票★，中方评委4人投票●

1. Wish you always keep a twinkle despite all the wrinkles.

(何冰 译) ★★★★

2. May you stay young upon your return.

(王梅兰 译) ●●

3. May you drift about half a life and return still young.

(杨秀波 译) ●●

4. May life only take you far, but not age your heart.

(吴春晓 译) ●●

5. May you return young after striving long.

(王成杰 译) ●●

6. May you be off half a life long and be back still young and strong.

(崔传明 译) ●●

7. Still youthful may you be, when you return after half your life sailing across the rough sea.

(张俊锋 译) ★

8. May you keep your youthful innocence even after a long and weary journey of life.

(刘雪芹 译) ★

9. May you still keep a sunny heart even if you are halfway through a trying life.

(石爱伟 译) ★

10. May you return still with a young heart even if you've been away half your life.

(魏红霞 译) ★

11. May you return with a heart still young after sailing in the ocean of life with waves high.

（王毅 译）★

第五篇　近现代时期

附录一
作者/著作索引

Appendix I
Author/Work Index

名言警句英译

名言警句英译

名言警句英译

附录二

句子索引

Appendix II
Sentence Index

哀莫大于心死。084

爱出者爱返，福往者福来。102

安而不忘危，存而不忘亡，治而不忘乱。003

安危不贰其志，险易不革其心。147

傲不可长，欲不可纵，志不可满，乐不可极。130

板凳需坐十年冷，文章不写一句空。317

邦以民为本，民以食为天，财者食之原。278

闭门即是深山，读书随处净土。251

兵无常势，水无常形。062

博学而笃志，切问而近思。048

不饱食以终日，不弃功于寸阴。139

不经一番寒彻骨，怎得梅花扑鼻香。187

不立异以为高，不逆情以干誉。193

不谋全局者，不足谋一域。306

不忘故乡，仁也；不恋本土，达也。146

不要人夸好颜色，只留清气满乾坤。234

不以规矩，不能成方圆。079

不义而富且贵，于我如浮云。051

不在其位，不谋其政。041

不责人小过，不发人阴私，不念人旧恶。267

不知而自以为知，百祸之宗也。096

不著一字，尽得风流。186

仓廪实则知礼节，衣食足则知荣辱。011

曾经沧海难为水，除却巫山不是云。183

成大事者，以识为主，以才为辅。294

乘人之车者载人之患，衣人之衣者怀人之忧，食人之食者死人之事。112

宠辱不惊，闲看庭前花开花落；去留无意，漫随天外云卷云

名言警句英译

穷则独善其身，达则兼济天下。076

求利当求国民利，求名当求身后名。312

曲高和寡，妙技难工。132

人不劝不善，钟不打不鸣。272

人固有一死，或重于泰山，或轻于鸿毛。122

人生万事须自为，跬步江山即寥廓。232

人生自古谁无死，留取丹心照汗青。223

人有悲欢离合，月有阴晴圆缺，此事古难全。200

人有不为也，而后可以有为。080

人有三个基本错误是不能犯的：一是德薄而位尊，二是智小而谋大，三是力小而任重。321

人之聪明，多失于浮炫。236

人之患，在好为人师。075

日日行，不怕千万里；常常做，不怕千万事。301

塞翁失马，焉知非福。103

三人行，必有我师焉；择其善者而从之，其不善者而改之。032

山不在高，有仙则名；水不在深，有龙则灵。181

山无陵，天地合，乃敢与君绝。206

山重水复疑无路，柳暗花明又一村。210

上下同欲者胜，风雨同舟者兴。064

少年读书，如隙中窥月；中年读书，如庭中望月；老年读书，如台上玩月。275

身无彩凤双飞翼，心有灵犀一点通。185

慎终如始，则无败事。019

慎终追远，民德归厚矣。052

圣人择可言而后言，择可行而后行。013

师者，所以传道受业解惑也。169

诗是无形画，画是有形诗。192

食必常饱，然后求美；衣必常暖，然后求丽；居必常安，然后求乐。114

士人有百折不回之真心，才有万变不穷之妙用。255

士为知己者死，女为悦己者容。115

世有伯乐，然后有千里马，千里马常有，而伯乐不常有。172

事不可做尽，言不可道尽，势不可倚尽，福不可享尽。303

事以密成，语以泄败。095

是非终日有，不听自然无。271

是故百战百胜，非善之善者也；不战而屈人之兵，善之善者也。065

是故弟子不必不如师，师不必贤于弟子，闻道有先后，术业有专攻，如是而已。174

恃大而不戒，则轻敌而屡败；知小而自畏，则深谋而必克。205

室雅何须大，花香不在多。279

树欲静而风不止，子欲养而亲不待。100

水激石则鸣，人激志则宏。308

水至清则无鱼，人至察则无徒。124

所谓大学者，非谓有大楼之谓也，有大师之谓也。313

所谓伊人，在水一方。010

泰山不让土壤，故能成其大；河海不择细流，故能就其深。097

天不言而四时行，地不语而百物生。157

天地不仁，以万物为刍狗。021

天将降大任于斯人也，必先苦其心志，劳其筋骨，饿其体肤，空乏其身，行拂乱其所为，所以动心忍性，增益其所不能。081

天生我材必有用，千金散尽还复来。154

天时不如地利，地利不如人和。072

天下皆知取之为取，而莫知与之为取。141

天下难事，必作于易；天下大事，必作于细。026

天下熙熙，皆为利来；天下攘攘，皆为利往。111

天下之事，常成于困约，而败于奢靡。212

天之道，利而不害；人之道，为而弗争。018

天之道，损有余而补不足。人之道则不然，损不足以奉有余。024

天作孽，犹可违；自作孽，不可活。004

投我以木桃，报之以琼瑶。008

万物各得其和以生，各得其养以成。091

往者不可谏，来者犹可追。043

为天地立心，为生民立命，为往圣继绝学，为万世开太平。198

为者常成，行者常至。069

位卑未敢忘忧国，事定犹须待阖棺。215

文章本天成，妙手偶得之。214

文章合为时而著，歌诗合为事而作。176

文章千古事，得失寸心知。165

文章做到极处，无有他奇，只是恰好；人品做到极处，无有他异，只是本然。269

问君能有几多愁，恰似一江春水向东流。189

问世间情为何物，直教人生死相许。220

我劝天公重抖擞，不拘一格降人才。291

我生本无乡，心安是归处。180

吾观自古贤达人，功成不退皆殒身。160

吾日三省吾身：为人谋而不忠乎？与朋友交而不信乎？传不习乎？034

梧桐一叶落，天下尽知秋。104

物忌全盛，事忌全美，人忌全名。246

物来顺应，未来不迎。当时不杂，既过不恋。298

喜名者必多怨，好誉者必多侮。101

名言警句英译

月满则亏，水满则溢。284

运用之妙，存乎一心。237

在天愿作比翼鸟，在地愿为连理枝。177

朝闻道，夕死可矣。047

政之所兴在顺民心，政之所废在逆民心。014

知人者智，自知者明。胜人者有力，自胜者强。015

知者乐水，仁者乐山。031

知足不辱，知止不殆。028

知足常足，终身不辱；知止常止，终身不耻。302

志高则言洁，志大则辞弘，志远则旨永。262

志合者，不以山海为远，道乖者，不以咫尺为近。137

志士不饮盗泉之水，廉者不受嗟来之食。143

志于道德者，功名不足累其心；志于功名者，富贵不足以累其心。243

致虚极，守静笃。万物并作，吾以观其复。029

智者千虑必有一失，愚者千虑必有一得。105

重剑无锋，大巧不工。323

朱门酒肉臭，路有冻死骨。166

最是人间留不住，朱颜辞镜花辞树。310

做学问要在不疑处有疑，待人要在有疑处不疑。315

"百人百译"团队
"A Hundred Translators,
a Hundred Translations" Team

中方投票评委（按 2022 年 12 月前投票次数排列）

郝晓燕	杨红东	张 硕	陶国霞	冯 奇	姜是是	王爱玲
李鹏辉	朱义华	朱文婷	陶悦馨	梁颖萍	刘 韬	赵雪丽
王金宇	侯 涛	霍 红	赵靖岩	晋旭生	蒋楚楚	李言实
刘锦峰	卫春燕	郝 玫	李红丽	卢绍刚	赵雪霞	吴润厦

外方投票评委（按 2022 年 12 月前投票次数排列）

Mark Awe Tachega	Maurice Lineman	Erick Dunham
Shaunice McLennon	Jared Hughes	Akoto Eugene
Jen Zhao	Michael Lue	Shadab Abdul Samir
Brandon Heart	Rose Adiba Afrah	Marleena Valfale
Adrian Lindsay	Thomas Starky	Helen Chou-Lee
Aghadiuno Francess	Stephen Lawrence	Richard Liu
Fabio Valfale	Ray Zhao	Mia Fraser
Russell White	Nicholas Breznick	Vaulmore Mack
Lana Delerue	Emily Weaver	

译者团队（按 2022 年 12 月前提交译文次数排列）

冯 雷	王昌玲	倪庆行	王绍昌	叶如钢	张晓阳	石爱伟
郁序新	任诚刚	杨秀波	石永浩	王成杰	王 毅	陶家乐

魏红霞	杨中仁	吴春晓	马建军	何　艳	艾朝阳	王梅兰
董秀静	乐国斌	樊功生	曹小菁	铁　冰	丁如伟	孙玲玲
董庆瑗	杨胜悦	张立国	张俊峰	田　璐	李开林	王如利
崔传明	何　冰	刘　群	王　婷	彭智鹏	华　卫	赵宜忠
张　晔	刘向军	钱朝晖	史红霞	邢　珈	刘德江	关恩亮
叶步青	瑞　雪	程永生	王慧玉	马百亮	张　莹	李红雨
刘雪芹	张　琼	丁立群	郑晓春	王　薇	陈光华	陈金金
李少波	马金龙	吴伟雄	王　勤	袁浩龙	伍敏毓	孟朝岗
孙　壮	张建惠	史潘荣	张小琴	闫晓宇	丁后银	徐艺玮
延　芳	赖祎华	张立峰	陈赛花	许霖越	王　琳	李　慧
陈　良	张顺生	段冰知	于元元	田　霞	王国己	颜海峰
陈丽珠	魏建国					

百人百译团队成员（部分）

曹小菁　天津市武清区精进引领文化信息咨询中心
崔传明　山东科技大学
丁后银　宿迁学院
丁立群　山东农业大学
丁如伟　华中师范大学
董庆瑗　苏州新教育学校
董秀静　太原工业学院
樊功生　香港中文大学
冯　雷　太原理工大学
郝晓燕　太原理工大学
何　冰　加拿大多伦多兰儿教育公司
何　艳　上海交通大学
晋旭生　山西大学
乐国斌　怀化学院

李开林　太原理工大学

李少波　成都东软学院

李正拴　河北师范大学

李　治　太原理工大学

刘向军　上海财经大学

刘雪芹　广西民族大学

马百亮　上海海洋大学

马建军　大连理工大学

倪庆行　山东农业大学

任诚刚　云南农业大学

石爱伟　忻州师范学院

史红霞　山西农业大学

石永浩　山东财经大学

陶国霞　浙江外国语学院

田　璐　广东外语外贸大学

铁　冰　广州市农业科学研究院

王昌玲　安徽师范大学

王成杰　大连交通大学

王慧玉　国防科技大学

王梅兰　加拿大多伦多兰儿教育公司

王如利　中央民族大学

王绍昌　美国达拉斯领英科文学院

王　婷　山西农业大学

王　薇　北京交通大学

王　毅　山西农业大学

魏红霞　安徽工程大学

吴春晓　大连民族大学

吴伟雄　北京理工大学珠海学院

伍敏毓　益阳职业技术学院

邢　珊　天津市武清区精进引领文化信息咨询中心

杨秀波　桂林理工大学

杨中仁　电子科技大学中山学院

叶如钢　美国加州大学圣巴巴拉分校

郁序新　苏州恒丰进出口有限公司

袁浩龙　厦门大学（学生）

张金萍　太原理工大学

张俊锋　上海理工大学

张立国　加拿大麦克马斯特大学

张顺生　上海理工大学

张　硕　西北师范大学

张晓阳　央媒资深媒体人

张　莹　天津职业大学

张智中　南开大学

赵雪丽　山西中医药大学

艾瑞克·邓汉姆（Erick Dunham）美国

贾瑞德·修斯（Jared Hughes）美国

拉塞尔·怀特（Russell White）英国

马　静（Shaunice McLennon）牙买加

马克·奥·塔其佳（Mark Awe Tachega）加纳

莫里斯·莱曼（Maurice Lineman）加拿大

尼古拉斯·不莱茨尼克（Nicholas Breznick）美国

斯蒂芬·劳伦斯（Stephen Lawrence）英国

王聪力（Adrian Lindsay）牙买加

赵　蓁（Jen Zhao）澳大利亚